D1014631

THE

DEVIL

IN THE CITY

OF ANGELS

MY ENCOUNTERS WITH THE DIABOLICAL

THE
DEVIL
IN THE CITY
OF ANGELS

MY ENCOUNTERS WITH THE DIABOLICAL

Jesse Romero

TAN Books
Charlotte, North Carolina

Copyright © 2019 Jesse Romero

All rights reserved. With the exception of short excerpts used in critical review, no part of this work may be reproduced, transmitted, or stored in any form whatsoever without the prior written permission of the publisher.

Unless otherwise noted, Scripture quotations are from the Revised Standard Version of the Bible—Second Catholic Edition (Ignatius Edition), copyright © 2206 National Council of the Churches of Christ in the United States of America. Used by permission. All rights reserved.

Scripture texts marked NABRE are taken from the New American Bible, revised edition © 2010, 1991, 1986, 1970 Confraternity of Christian Doctrine, Washington, D.C. and are used by permission of the copyright owner. All rights reserved. No part of the New American Bible may be reproduced in any form without permission in writing from the copyright owner.

Scripture texts marked NIV are taken from the Holy Bible, New International Version, NIV Copyright © 1973, 1978, 1984, 2011 by Biblica, Inc. Used by permission. All rights reserved worldwide.

Excerpts from the English translation of the Catechism of the Catholic Church for use in the United States of America © 1994, United States Catholic Conference, Inc.—Libreria Editrice Vaticana. Used with permission.

Cover design by Caroline K. Green

Library of Congress Control Number: 2019938671

ISBN: 978-1-5051-1370-9

Published in the United States by
TAN Books
PO Box 410487
Charlotte, NC 28241
www.TANBooks.com

Printed in the United States of America

CONTENTS

FOREWORD

Today we are witnessing an unprecedented rise in the occult all over the world, even inside the Church; the evidence for which is overwhelming. Scripture tells us that at the end of the ages, there will be an acceleration of evil such as has never been seen before. Unfortunately, the devil has lulled the majority of people in the world to sleep, comfortable in the erroneous belief that he doesn't exist. In writing this book, Jesse Romero has done Holy Mother Church a great service because most Catholics get their information about spirits, angels, and demons from Hollywood movies and TV series.

Many people have had encounters with evil spirits and the diabolical, but because we have become more secular and less faithful, we are led to believe that demonic possession or simply an awareness of the devil is just a type of "mental illness" that can be cured with a pill or medication. Most people never talk about their personal encounters with evil spirits or demons because they are just too embarrassed to share these experiences for fear of being called "nuts" or "crazy." This subject is taboo, and most people that experience the diabolical whisper it to a confidant. Jesse Romero, a well-known bilingual Catholic lay evangelist, has dared to speak up, and in the pages that follow, he shares in detail his encounters with evil spirits and witches. His stories follow

St. Paul's exhortation to expose the darkness (see Eph 5:11) because "the days are evil" (Eph 5:16).

Read this book, inform yourself, stay close to Our Lord and Our Lady; they will be your first responders when you call upon them. We serve Mary, a twelve-star general (see Rv 12:1–5). Your "sword of the Spirit" (Eph 6:17) must be soaked in the blood of demons and dragons. Let's unite our souls and prayers to the heel of Our Blessed Mother, the Sword of St. Michael, and the Precious Powerful blood of Jesus so that we can deliver a powerful blow to Satan and his kingdom and send them reeling back to hell on judgment day.

Bishop Eduardo Nevares,
Auxiliary Bishop of the Diocese of Phoenix

INTRODUCTION

Why Did I Write This Book?

"**B**ecause one out of three (Catholic) theologians does not believe in the existence of Satan; almost two out of three believe in his existence but not in his practical actions and refuse to take it into account in pastoral activity. This leaves very little room for those who believe and try to act accordingly. The few exceptions are forced to act against the tide, and often are ridiculed and ostracized by the rest of the clergy. These statistics were gathered in West Germany in 1974 and were published in the Concilium."[1] Those who don't preach the truth from the pulpit about the reality of the devil and hell are guilty of "ecclesiastical malpractice." Those teachers who are cowardly preachers in this life, if they don't repent, will experience "climate change" in the next life.

It is not surprising that our clergy's failings and weaknesses have been laid bare for all to see in extreme fashion in recent months and years. Our Lady of Akita, Japan, said to Sr. Sasagawa in 1973 regarding the intensity of demons against our clergy:

---

[1]   Gabriele Amorth, *An Exorcist—More Stories* (San Francisco: Ignatius Press, 2002).

The work of the devil will infiltrate even into the Church in such a way that one will see cardinals opposing cardinals, bishops against bishops. The priests who venerate me will be scorned and opposed by their confreres . . . churches and altars sacked; the Church will be full of those who accept compromises and the demon will press many *priests and consecrated souls* to leave the service of the Lord. . . .The demon will be especially implacable against souls consecrated to God. The thought of the loss of so many souls is the cause of my sadness. If sins increase in number and gravity, there will be no longer pardon for them.[2]

Here is another reason I wrote this book: *Catholics don't believe in the devil!*

A recent study reveals that Catholics are among the least likely to agree that Satan is a "living being." That finding was published by the Center for Research on the Apostolate (CARA) at Georgetown University. A recent survey of 1,495 US adults who believe in God reveals that Evangelical Christians are nearly three times more likely than Catholics to believe that Satan is a "living being." Fifty-five percent of Evangelical Christians interviewed view Satan as an active and "cunning adversary" as described in the New Testament while only 17 percent of all Catholics polled indicated that they viewed Satan as a living presence in the world. Rather, Catholics are more likely to view Satan as a symbol of evil

---

2   "The Apparitions of the Blessed Virgin Mary in Akita, Japan, to Sr. Agnes Sasagawa," EWTN, November 2011, https://www.ewtn.com/library/mary/akita.htm.

rather than a "real" living being.[3] Contrast that with Catholic teaching as found within the *Catechism of the Catholic Church*, which describes Satan as a real being, specifically a fallen angel who rebelled against God (CCC 391–95).

Venerable Fulton Sheen observed more than fifty years ago that the Church's real problem was that "our theologians have neglected the demonic. . . . The demonic is always most powerful when he is denied. It is almost impossible today to find a theologian writing about the demonic, unless it be to deny it."[4] The problem is worse today . . . much worse.

In 2017, Cardinal Archbishop Charles Chaput of Philadelphia wrote the following of the Polish intellectual and convert Leszek Kolakowski:

> Exactly 30 years ago, Kolakowski gave a lecture at Harvard entitled 'The Devil in History.' . . . Kolakowski saw that we can't fully understand our culture unless we take the devil seriously. The devil and evil are constants at work in human history and in the struggles of every human soul. And note that Kolakowski (unlike some of our own Catholic leaders who should know better) was not using the word 'devil' as a symbol of the darkness in our own hearts, or a metaphor for the bad things that happen in the world. He was talking about the spiritual being Jesus called 'the evil

---

[3]   Anne Hendershott, "What, the Devil?" *Catholic World Report*, September 8, 2017, www.catholicworldreport.com/2017/09/08/what-the-devil/.

[4]   Fulton J. Sheen and Henry Dieterich, *Through the Year with Fulton Sheen: Inspirational Selections for Each Day of the Year* (San Francisco: Ignatius Press, 2003).

one' and 'the father of lies' — the fallen angel who works tirelessly to thwart God's mission and Christ's work of salvation. This is why the evangelization of culture is *always,* in some sense, a call to spiritual warfare. We're in a struggle for souls. Our adversary is the devil. And while Satan is not God's equal and doomed to final defeat, he can do bitter harm in human affairs. The first Christians knew this. We find their awareness written on nearly every page of the New Testament. The modern world makes it hard to believe in the devil. But it treats Jesus Christ the same way. And that's the point. Medieval theologians understood this quite well. They had an expression in Latin: *Nullus diabolus, nullus redemptor.* No devil, no Redeemer. Without the devil, it's very hard to explain why Jesus needed to come into the world to suffer and die for us. What exactly did he redeem us *from?* The devil, more than anyone, appreciates this irony, i.e., that we can't fully understand the mission of Jesus without him. And he exploits this to his full advantage. He knows that consigning him to myth inevitably sets in motion our same treatment of God.[5]

C. S. Lewis wrote a masterpiece on the diabolical that you should read if you have not already. In letter VII of his book *The Screwtape Letters,* the senior demon, who is named Screwtape, tells his young protégé, Wormwood, that the

---

[5]   Charles Chaput, "Sympathy for the Devil," *Catholic Philly,* June 5, 2017, catholicphilly.com/2017/06/think-tank/archbishop-cha-put-column/sympathy-for-the-devil/.

most effective thing he can do to bring souls to hell is to convince people that Satan does not even exist.[6] According to the above surveys, the devil's tactic, as imagined by one of the great Christian writers, is certainly working.

Fr. Gabriel Amorth, a Vatican Exorcist for thirty-three years, wrote, "Theology will be unfinished and incomprehensible until it focuses on the world of the angels. A Christology that ignores Satan is crippled and will never understand the magnitude of redemption."[7]

Saint John Paul II stated, "He who does not believe in the devil does not believe in the Gospel."[8]

Fr. Pedro Mendoza Pantoja, a leading exorcist in Mexico, commented, "What the devil is interested in is to confuse us, either by making us believe that he doesn't exist and that, since he doesn't exist, neither do hell and heaven."[9]

Fr. Gary Thomas, an exorcist, said, "The clash of forces between good and evil in society causes confusion."[10] Clearly many Catholics today are confused, so confused that they don't even believe in the devil anymore!

---

[6] Clive Staples Lewis, *The Screwtape Letters* (CrossReach Publications, 2016).

[7] Gabriele Amorth and Nicoletta V. MacKenzie, *An Exorcist Tells His Story* (Ignatius Press, 1999).

[8] Sd, "Famous Exorcist On How 'Smoke' Of Devil Entered Church," *Spirit Daily Blog*, May 27, 2017, spiritdaily.org/blog/uncategorized/famous-exorcist-on-how-smoke-of-devil-entered-church.

[9] "Satan's Strategy of Confusion (Part 2)," *ZENIT - English*, January, 1 2016, zenit.org/articles/satan-s-strategy-of-confusion-part-2/.

[10] Gary Thomas, lecture at St. Joseph's Church, Meadows, Diocese of San Jose, November 11, 2017.

Father Candido Amantini, a Passionist priest and Rome's chief exorcist for more than thirty years, asked a demon during an exorcism, "How many are you?" The demon responded, "We are so many that, if we were visible, we would darken the sun."[11]

If you are Catholic, you must know that the existence of demons is "de fide," defined dogma. The Fourth Lateran Council declared that "Satan and the other devils are (1) by nature spirits . . . (2) created by God, (3) and so originally good, (4) but fell into sin (5) of their own free will" and that they are (6) "eternally damned."

What about those people—perhaps most Catholics in fact—that do believe in the existence of the devil but still choose to live a faith which is lukewarm, tepid, and indifferent? Here is an anecdotal story for them.

> The Devil was being advised by his demons on how to steal souls to hell. The demons told the Devil, "Let's tell them there is no God." The Devil said, "They will never believe us; the knowledge of God is written in every human heart." The demons said, "Let's tell them there is no heaven or hell." The Devil said, "They will never believe that, they all know in the heart of hearts that there is a place outside of earth called heaven and hell." The demons said, "(We) know what to tell them, lets convince them that there is no hurry to convert, yeah, lets tell them there is no hurry, that they have

---

[11]   Gabriele Amorth, et al, *An Exorcist Explains the Demonic: the Antics of Satan and His Army of Fallen Angels* (Sophia Institute Press, 2016), 17.

a long life to live so they should just eat, drink and indulge in the world."

And for two thousand years, he has been lying to people by this great strategy concocted from hell, demons telling people there is no hurry to convert. And people have been listening. But let's stop listening to the devil and start listening to God! God tells us not to delay! It is right there in Scripture! Do we trust God's word?

"Do not delay to turn to the Lord, nor postpone it from day to day; for suddenly the wrath of the Lord will go forth, and at the time of punishment you will perish" (Sir 5:7).

"But God said to him, 'Fool! This night your soul is required of you; and the things you have prepared, whose will they be?'" (Lk 12:20).

"Just as it is appointed that human beings die once, and after this the judgment" (Heb 9:27 NABRE).

THE DEVIL

Who Is the Devil?

The devil is one of the legion of evil spirits who were originally good angels created by God but who made themselves evil by refusing to obey the will of God.

The devil (from *diabolus*, meaning slanderer) and demons are fallen angels whose leader is Satan (adversary). In both the Old and the New Testaments, Satan is the enemy of God, who brings about evil and tempts human beings to defy God's laws. Even Jesus allowed himself to be tempted by Satan in the desert. *Why? To give us an example of how to resist him and how to fight back.*

References to the devil are frequent in the Scriptures. Their prominent feature is that a personal, malicious force is active in the world. It is deliberately bent on preventing the designs of God.

Why Is the Devil Allowed to Tempt Us?

The final explanation of why Satan is allowed to tempt us is a mystery. But divine revelation gives us several profound reasons why God allows this.

- By our resistance of the evil spirit, we prove our loyalty to God. There is such a thing as being tested in order to more deeply and clearly understand God's providence in our lives.
- The devil's purpose is, of course, malicious. But God allows the evil spirit to tempt us so that we may grow in our love for God.

The following is my synopsis of Venerable Mary of Ágreda's account of the fall of Lucifer from her book *The Mystical City of God*.

This information on Lucifer comes from Sacred Tradition, Holy Scripture, and from the writings of Venerable Maria de Jesus of Ágreda, Spain (1602–1665). The Blessed Virgin Mary dictated to this Spanish nun the entire story of her (the Blessed Mother's) life which the nun wrote down in a very comprehensive volume titled *The Mystical City of God*. This mystical city is actually the body of the Virgin Mary in which God the Son lived for nine months. And wherever God the Son lives, there too is God the Father and God the Holy Spirit. In only a few short months after you and I die, our bodies will rot in the grave. The body of this Spanish nun can be seen incorrupt in her convent in Ágreda, Spain. Sister Maria de Jesus died almost 350 years ago, and her body lies and looks exactly the same today as on the day she died without any help from modern science. This miracle of God lends credibility to all that she wrote.

Lucifer was the most beautiful of all the creatures created by God. The name "Lucifer" (Is 14:12) means bright star, bright being. Of all the angels created by God as pure spirits without a body and with a free will, Lucifer was by far the most brilliant, the most intelligent, and the most powerful. Unfortunately, through this gift of free will, Lucifer, like so many of us, chose to become the most prideful, most arrogant, and the most envious creature. Consequently, he chose to become the most horrible creature in all of God's creation. All the angels are spiritual beings created by God with an abundance of knowledge, understanding, and power. All these divine gifts notwithstanding, they are still creatures and *not* God. This is a detail that Lucifer, his minions, and many times we humans choose to forget. We humans often times forget that we are mere creatures that owe everything to our God.

Lucifer and all of the angels were created in that one instant when God said, "Let there be light" (Gn 1:3). In that instant, they were created as bright beings of light. But even though they had been created in God's heaven, they had not yet been allowed to see God. All the angels were, just like all of us here on earth, on a sort of trial. They were being tested and would have to earn the privilege of seeing the Beatific Vision by passing this test of obedience to God. God gave them all the information that they needed in stages and not all at once so that they could make the proper choice of freely choosing to serve God for all eternity. Lucifer and all the other angels were even informed of the consequences of disobedience. They were told that a place of fire and eternal punishment would be created to punish any who chose not to obey and serve God. But it seems that just as so many of us choose to ignore this inevitable consequence of our bad actions we call hell, Lucifer and one third of all the angels (see Rv 12:4) chose to believe that a God so benevolent would not also be all-just and punish disobedience. In their sin of pride, they created for themselves a false image of the Creator, an image designed to suit *their* selfish desires. Sadly, so many of us humans do this as well.

In the beginning, however, Lucifer was in complete accord with God. But then after Lucifer was "given the blueprints," so to speak, for the creation of man as an inferior being to the angels with a body, flesh, and a soul, but was told that he, the greatest angel of them all, would have to kneel before and serve God the Son in human form, Lucifer's love of self, and the sins of pride and envy, got the better of him. The last straw came when Lucifer was told that he and all the angels would have to serve the Queen of Heaven, Mary the mother of Jesus. Lucifer rebelled against God and convinced one third of all the angels to serve, obey, and worship him rather than God. The sad truth is that Lucifer forgot that he was a mere creature when he demanded that God give to him the place that was reserved exclusively for Jesus the Christ.

Lucifer and his unfaithful minions in their act of rebellion went from being the most beautiful to the most horrible creatures in God's creation: Satan and his malignant devils. But even in their current hideous state, they did not lose their knowledge, cunning, and power. The job of casting all these devils into hell was accorded by God to Saint Michael the Archangel, who, together with all the faithful angels, won the first war that ever took place in heaven. As our Lady of Fatima told us, war is a punishment for sin.

The tremendous hatred and envy that Satan and his demons have for all of humanity has no equal in all of creation. This hatred stems from the fact that we humans can still reach the heaven that Satan and his devils lost for all eternity. This is why Satan tempts us with the seven capital sins: pride, envy, wrath, sloth, greed, gluttony, and lust. While pride offends God the most, it is lust that sends the most souls to hell. Beware of the sins of lust. This admonition, too, came from our Lady of Fatima in Portugal in 1917.

Satan's greatest victory over all humanity is getting most humans in every generation to believe that he (Satan) and hell do not exist. This lie, when carried to its end rationale, leads humans to the erroneous conclusion that neither do God and heaven exist. Thus, we are free of any punitive consequences for our foul and sinful deeds. This lie is what gives individuals, at least in their own minds, license to embrace and wholeheartedly support the culture of death: artificial birth control (which is the mother that spawned this culture of death), abortion, euthanasia, mercy killing, doctor and pharmacist assisted suicide, drug use, abuse, and trafficking, wanton murders, worldwide terrorism, and homosexuality.[12]

Hispanic Catholics – Will We Be Servants of Christ or Servants of Satan?

Catholics—but most especially Hispanic or Latino Catholics—are being vexed, harassed, annoyed, and targeted by

---

[12]   María de Jesús and Geo J. Blatter, *The Mystical City of God: the Divine History and Life of the Virgin Mother of God, Our Queen and Our Lady, Most Holy Mary, Expiatrix of the Fault of Eve and Mediatrix of Grace ; the Miracle of His Omnipotence and the Abyss of His Grace* (TAN Books, 2013).

Satanism, Santeria, Santa Muerte, and witchcraft. If Hispanic Catholics are going to be used as God's Delta Force in the new evangelization, then we need to be equipped against these dangerous destructive occultic groups who are preying on us. Bishop Thomas J. Olmsted, during opening remarks at the October 28, 2017 event held at St. Paul Parish, said, "But in 2017 the largest group in the Catholic Church in America are Hispanics and Latinos."[13] Hispanic evangelization must include exposing the deceptions of the occult groups which have made such inroads in the Hispanic Catholic community. I speak from personal experience as you will see in the pages that follow.

---

[13]   Tony Gutierrez, "Millennials seek meaningful relationships, sense of welcoming," *The Catholic Sun*, vol. 33, no.11, November 16, 2017, p. 1.

2

MY ENCOUNTERS WITH THE DIABOLICAL

Perhaps, to many people, the stories that follow will seem "out of this world" or exaggerated. At the very least, I will grant that they are beyond the common experiences of many individuals. That said, I can attest that each and every one is true and happened as I describe it below. One sees things as a sheriff's deputy that most people are not exposed to, thankfully. And in the barrios of East Los Angeles (ELA) and other areas where Hispanic culture is dominant, paths to Satan are all too prevalent through the cults of Santeria and Santa Muerte. My hope in sharing these stories is that whoever reads this book will learn something of the terrifying power of Satan and be scared straight and never dabble in the occult. It is not a game, as you will see. However, just as importantly, I hope to convey the truth that the surest way to avoid the devil and his power is to stay close to Jesus Christ and his bride, the Catholic Church. Receive the sacraments as often as possible and live in a state of grace. God bless you all.[14]

---

[14] The names of those involved in the incidents below have been changed or masked to protect their privacy.

Encounters With Demons

Mentally Ill Offenders Unit—First Encounter

In 1983, while working as a rookie Los Angeles deputy sheriff in the LA County Jail, the largest in the world, I was escorting prisoners to a section of the jail called the Mentally Ill Offenders Unit (MIOU). That is where they kept all the serial killers, mass murderers, psychopaths, and sociopaths. Most of them had satanic tattoos and satanic bibles along with pornography in their one-man cells. Out of curiosity, I would read the police reports, probation reports, and psychological evaluations detailing the gory macabre crimes committed by these "lifers" (life in prison) or death row inmates housed in the Mentally Ill Offenders Unit of the jail.

One day while at work inside the jail, a Bible verse suddenly came to mind that I had heard a few Sundays prior at Holy Mass. It was 1 Corinthians 12:3, which reads, "Therefore I want you to understand that no one speaking by the Spirit of God ever says, 'Jesus be cursed!' and no one can say 'Jesus is Lord' except by the Holy Spirit." While at work, I kept thinking about this verse, and as I walked up and down the row of cells at the MIOU, I observed a lot of these high security inmates (in single man cells) talking to someone in their jail cell that was not there, a figment of their imagination perhaps. I noticed bizarre behavior: some of them were constantly shaking, some were howling and growling, some were in yoga positions with their bodies shaped like a pretzel, seemingly in a catatonic state, some looked as if they were in a trance with their eyes rolled back, some just stared with a look that was pure evil and rage, their eyes all black, with neither pupil nor iris. Some were so violent and erratic they were tied down with leather restraints on a bed and sedated with medication every few hours.

As I was doing my prisoner cell count (every twenty minutes), I walked to this one prisoner's cell who had murdered an entire family in his neighborhood and then cannibalized them. He was a self-proclaimed Satanist with numerous satanic tattoos (666, a goat's head, an inverted cross, a dragon, a pentagram, etc.). He had just been convicted of mass murder with special circumstances (cannibalism), and we were ready to ship him off to death row in a week or so. I put my face between the bars, and I talked to him with respect. I asked him if he was hungry, and he said yes. I asked him if he could say "Jesus is Lord." I told him that if he did so, I would go down to the officers' kitchen and bring him food from the officers' dining room (they served us great food). I told him I would bring a large portion of chicken, a huge pastrami sandwich, or a large chili cheeseburger and fries. I knew he would appreciate this offer because all he had eaten for the last two years was generic, bland inmate jail food prepared in bulk. This death row inmate smiled and said, "Sure thing, Deputy." I said "OK, go ahead and say, 'Jesus is Lord.'" He said, "No problem," and he began earnestly trying to say it because he wanted to eat a good meal, but he physically could not. It was as if his mouth was shut closed with tape or he had cement in his mouth; he was physically trying to speak those sacred words, but all he could do was grunt and growl. He turned as red as an apple and then started holding his neck as if something was choking him. His countenance became very angry and ugly as he forcefully grunted and tried to say the words I had asked him to. I felt a cold chill like an ice cube go down my back, and then I felt the entire temperature drop like a refrigerator in the hallway. A cold breeze came from his jail cell that seemed to cover me. I walked away backwards very slowly from the cell of this Satanic inmate. I was startled and surprised. I said to myself, "Wow, the Bible is right." I had just witnessed a satanic mass murderer who was physically unable to say "Jesus is Lord."

This is one of many times in my career as a Los Angeles deputy sheriff where inmates in this particular section of the LA County Jail (the Mentally Ill Offenders Unit) could not say the name of Jesus after I made them the same offer of bringing them a thanksgiving meal. It's as if something invisible clutched all of them at their throats and they would begin choking as they attempted to say the sacred words "Jesus is Lord."

On another occasion, I talked to Richard Ramirez, "the night stalker" who haunted southern California by killing thirteen women and doing unspeakable things to their bodies during the attack and after the attack. He actually boasted of killing many more women that he was never prosecuted for. In his jail cell, he had a "satanic bible," which he read every day, and a stack of pornographic magazines about two to three feet high. His conscience was dead, no doubt as a result of what he read. The satanic bible and pornography were the only things he read. After he was convicted of multiple murders in superior court and was then free to talk about his case, he told me that he had been ordered to kill these women by Satan, whom he called his father. He would admit this quite readily to the deputy sheriffs in jail (after he was convicted). He had the tattoo of a pentagram on his hand, and on his way out of court everyday, he would flash his tattoo and make satanic signs with his hands (the devil's horns) for the cameras every day. This is known as perfect possession, when the person makes a pact with the devil with his intellect and will.

"'Perfect possession' is supposedly when an evil entity has taken such total control of a person that there is not even an indication that a person has an inner demon—no sign of struggle, not on the surface, just a general evilness. A person who is 'perfectly possessed' would seem at ease with his or her evil, or simply and fully indifferent to it."[15]

Diabolical subjugation or dependence is the classic Faustian bargain or pact with the devil. In Fr. Gabriel Amorth's words, "People fall into this form of evil when they voluntarily submit to Satan. The two most common forms of dependence are the blood pact with the devil and the consecration to Satan." Fr. Malachi Martin called this total or *perfect possession*. Since the human, with full consent and assent, voluntarily invites in the demon(s), we would not expect the totally (perfectly) possessed person to seek an exorcist. In other words, the cases of demonic possession that come to the attention of exorcists are only of the partial or incomplete variety, which is a frightening thought.

---

[15]   Michael H. Brown, "Question of the Week: Can the Leader of a Nation Become 'Perfectly Possessed?'" *Spirit Daily,* www.spiritdaily.org/perfectpossession.htm.

I believe that the vast majority of the sociopaths and psychopathic serial killers and mass murderers that I saw in the L.A. County Jail were perfectly possessed.

Saturday Night Family Disturbance Call—Second Encounter

The following encounter with the diabolical took place when I was working night shift (6 p.m. to 2 a.m.) in East Los Angeles. It was about midnight on a busy Saturday night. My partner and I got a call for service by the dispatcher. It was a 415F, 415D, 390S (family fight, disturbance, people drunk, loud music, neighbors complaining). My partner and I were a few blocks away from these apartment complexes in a rough neighborhood. We arrived and ran up the stairs and knocked on the apartment door. We could hear people grunting and being physical with each other (it sounded like a wrestling match). An old lady, seemingly an "abuela" or grandmother, opened the door and was very happy to see us. She said that her grandson was out of control, that he was attacking everybody, cursing and destroying the interior of the house. She told me, "Esta endemoniado" (he has a demon or he is possessed).

She invited us in, and what I saw caused me to rub my eyeballs. There was a young teen (fourteen or fifteen years old) on his back. He was being restrained by four adult men, who were each holding an arm and a leg, and he was growling like a dog, baring his teeth. His body was shaking violently, he was spitting, scratching, and biting, he had no pupil or iris, and his eyes were completely white. He was speaking a language that I didn't understand; it was not Spanish. The men were yelling, "Esta fuerte, esta fuerte," which translates, "He's strong, he's strong." In Spanish, I twice told the men holding this teen, "Sheriff's department, let him go." They let him go and his body remained in a supine position about twelve inches off the ground. My partner and I got down on the floor to see what was holding him up, and he was simply levitating in the air for a few seconds before the men pushed him down again. The grandmother told me in Spanish, "Officer, he talks with the devil in his room every night." She grabbed something from the dining table, and she handed me a board game; it was a Ouija board. She told me that he plays with that board every night. My partner knew I was a practicing Catholic, and he asked me, "What do we do? Do we call for backup?" I said, "No, we need to pray." He said, "That's not part of our academy training." The young teen, who was now on his back on the floor, got on all fours like a dog and began attacking the men. I ordered all the men, "Start praying and don't stop! Pray with faith!"

The pious grandmother knew exactly what to do, and she began leading everybody in the holy Rosary in a loud exuberant voice. I am sure everybody in the apartment complex could hear us. I told another family member to give me a rosary, give me holy water, give me blessed objects. Within seconds, the family was handing me rosaries, miraculous medals, scapulars, and holy water. My partner stood at the door with his hand on his gun. He was a fallen away Catholic and was completely bewildered and overwhelmed by what he was seeing. I began doing deliverance prayers over the teen; over and over I was praying the St. Michael the Archangel prayer, the Anima Christi prayer, and mostly spontaneous prayers ordering the evil spirit to leave this young man in the name and in the power of Jesus through the intercession of Our Lady. I was ordering this evil spirit to leave him and go to the foot of the cross in Jesus's name and by Jesus's authority. *I had been taught to pray like this not by the Los Angeles Sheriff's Academy class 213, but by my parents.*

We bathed that room in prayer nonstop, all of us. I was fully enveloped in sweat from the intensity of my prayers, my own nervousness of the situation, and what I was actually witnessing. The teen's face seemed to change into a dark ugly monstrous face and then come back to a normal human face. We battled in prayer; I drenched him with holy water and consecrated him with every sacramental and medal to Jesus through Mary that we had by draping them around his neck.

After about forty minutes, he stopped fighting, stopped thrashing, stopped growling, stopped cursing, fell limp, and became silent. I told the family to keep on praying. The young teen opened his eyes and ran over to hug his grandmother and began weeping. He said, "The monster is gone. He's gone; he left me." I sat down with the teen and gave him a quick heart to heart talk on being a friend of God and living in a state of grace. I told him about the dangers of the Ouija board, and he agreed with me. He told me he did not want that monster to come back inside of him, and I told him that he has to go to Mass with his grandmother every Sunday, sign up for confirmation, and go to confession immediately. I told the family to take him to see a Catholic priest the next day for confession and to sign him up for confirmation.

That night, my partner and I drove to the San Gabriel Mountains with the Ouija board and burned it to ashes; the wind scattered them into night. As a result of that incident, my partner came back to the practice of his Catholic faith. He asked me how I knew what to do since we had never been trained on how to deal with something like that. I told him when you come back to the practice of your Catholic faith, the Holy Spirit will lead you, guide you, and give you wisdom. I didn't tell my partner that my parents had been talking to me and teaching me (for several years) about engaging in spiritual warfare and being bold and unafraid and trusting in the power of the Lord and the intercession of Our Lady.

Demons are very legalistic; they know when they have permission to enter and torment a person and they know when they don't have permission to enter.

What's at play here is the law of invitation and the law of attraction:

- Demons are either invited by the victim
- or demons are attracted to people who are evil and or those lost souls who habitually live in mortal sin. (A powerful motivator to confess your mortal sins quickly!)

What is the point of entry? The above case falls under the law of invitation; this young man played with fire and, perhaps inadvertently, invited a demon by using a Ouija board.

911 Call: Shots Fired—Third Encounter

My partner and I were working the Cudahy night shift; this city had the highest concentration of parolees (ex-convicts) of any city in Los Angeles County. It was a 911 call, "shots fired" inside a house; we were assigned the call, arrived within five minutes, and had backup on the way. We approached the front door, announced "Sheriff's department," and entered the house with our weapons drawn ready to engage an armed suspect. We encountered an older lady in her late fifties or early sixties with a shotgun in her arms sitting on a chair in the living room next to an older man who was just shot in the head. His head was blown completely off his body. The body of the male sat on the chair, blood oozing from the severed head; ligaments, muscle, and bone were protruding from where his head used to be.

We ordered her to drop the gun; she offered no resistance. We grabbed the shotgun away from her and it was quite obvious that she had shot her husband. Under United States law, we are innocent until proven guilty, so I asked her, "Who did this? Where are they?"

She responded, "He told me to."

I said, "Who did?" She said, "He's right there in the corner. Don't you see him? He's laughing, he's laughing." Right when she said that, I felt the room get cold, as if we had stepped into a walk-in freezer at a restaurant, and the house smelled like fecal matter. We placed her under arrest immediately and took her to the patrol car. She kept looking at the corner of the living room and talking to an invisible person in a language that I had never heard before. We called paramedics and homicide. We left the crime scene to the detectives and drove back to the sheriff station in East LA with the female suspect handcuffed in the back seat of our patrol car.

There is a cage that separates the suspects from the officers in a patrol car, and I am glad there is because I was particularly spooked by this woman. I kept thinking about that invisible person in her living room that she kept looking at and talking to. As we drove to the sheriff station and I was asking her basic information in order to fill out my booking slip (the reception document to process an arrestee into the jail system), she was not very cooperative; she was talking to herself or someone else in the back seat with her. She could not focus on my simple questions and was incoherent.

In between her rambling, she became coherent and told me and my partner, "I had to do it. The devil told me to. I had to. He told me to." Then she would switch gears and begin talking to someone else in the back seat (who was not there since she was alone). She was telling this invisible entity, "Did I do good? Did you like what I did to him? Did I do good? Are you happy?" Then she would start speaking unknown languages; she would start growling and barking like a ferocious dog. I turned around to look at her, and I noticed that her eyes were completely white, no iris or pupil were present. She appeared to be in a trance and she would shake uncontrollably and shake her head left and right over and over again very quickly. My partner, who was a fallen away Catholic, asked me, "Is she crazy or is she possessed?"

I said probably both and started praying in my mind prayers of protection for both of us in the patrol car. I felt a real evil presence coming from her. She leaned forward and put her mouth right up to the cage that separates officers from suspects, and she looked at both of us with only the whites of her eyes and began saying, "Chop, chop, chop, cut, cut, cut, chop, chop, chop, cut, cut, cut." She repeated this over and over again as she looked at me and my partner. My partner later told me (what I felt), that he sensed a strong presence of something very evil that came from her or within her.

We arrived at the Sheriff Station and put her in a jail cell. I went to the report writing room and checked to see if she had a criminal record. She did. I discovered that she was a career criminal, was on parole, and had done prison time for several aggravated assaults with a knife and scissors some years ago. I know most cops would simply say, "Oh, she's just a 5150" (which means "crazy" in LA law enforcement jargon). This woman had a dead conscience, and I have no doubt that she had aligned her will with the will of Satan. She was simply carrying out the work of that murderer and liar. This was an extreme example of the article from the Catechism that tells us that "ignorance of God is the principle and explanation of all moral deviations" (CCC 2087).

What was the point of entry? Demons are attracted to evil people. I believe this was another case of perfect possession. She probably aligned her will to the will of Satan through a pact.

Suicide and Satanism—Fourth Encounter

My godson Salvador told me about a friend of his named Andy that needed help. Andy had been a great athlete in high school, a high-level baseball player who had a very promising future. In fact, he was already being scouted by professional baseball teams right out of high school. However, he had also been smoking marijuana since he was ten years old, yet he was able to hide it well and perform at a high physical level because of his youth and natural abilities.

Andy was asked to try out for a farm league team; he went to the tryouts and passed with flying colors. He was assured that he would be picked up by an MLB team within a year or two. Andy envisioned himself being rich and famous by the time he was twenty-four or twenty-five. His future certainly looked promising. However, Andy was a fallen away Catholic; he was a secular humanist and a daily marijuana smoker. As an aside, Venerable Fulton Sheen said in the 1970s in a lecture entitled "A Voice from Calvary" that the demon of drugs and marijuana is named "Bachus" (*whom I reject and renounce in Jesus's name*).

The scouts from the farm team connected to the MLB teams paid a surprise visit to Andy in East LA. They told him that before he went to camp in Arizona for spring training, he had to provide a urine sample because they wanted to make sure he was not using illegal drugs. Andy was surprised by this visit; the scouts followed him to the bathroom to watch him urinate into the plastic bottle. A week later, the baseball scouts called up Andy and told him that all bets were off. They had found marijuana, cocaine, and meth in his system. His baseball career was over before it started. Andy, who had just turned nineteen, was devastated and felt that his whole life came crashing down upon him.

He went into a full-blown depression for the next two and a half years. He continued using drugs every day, quit his job at the local supermarket, and had no desire to go back to school (college, that is). He became so angry with everyone that his personality became toxic. He was given bad advice by some low information person in his neighborhood who sent him to a witch.[16] He was told that this witch could change his fortune and change his future. The witch told him that she could give him powers to curse and hurt those people that canceled his baseball contract.

Andy went to a black satanic mass and gave his life to the devil. He said he was baptized naked in a pot of hot oil and was ordered to make a profession of faith to Satan. He said several women were dancing around him naked for two hours chanting words he could not understand. A satanic priest danced around him and poured oils over him as they laid their hands on him and spoke incantations over him in a language he did not understand.

After this experience, he began attending a satanic coven for the next two years every week, sometimes more often. He participated in many animal sacrifices and drank from many chalices containing animal and human blood. He even shaved his head and put a tattoo of a goat's head and a pentagram on top of his head (that is the mark of Satan).

---

16   For more information about the role of witches or "brujas" in Hispanic communities, read about my encounters with some of them in the latter half of chapter 2 .

He was told that if he participated in all these satanic rituals, he would have power over his enemies and he would be able to change the minds of the baseball scouts through mental telepathy. Andy was all in; he painted his room pitch black and listened to dark, profane, disordered music all day long.

His parents said he went from bad to worse and became increasingly violent. Between the ages of nineteen and twenty-one, he punched holes in every wall in the house and broke every door, table, and chair. He would attack his parents, and they would have to run out of the house in order to find safety at which time they were forced to call the sheriff's department several times. They would come and take him to jail and commit him for seventy-two hours of observation in a hospital psychiatric ward. It was at this point that I got involved as my godson told Andy's parents that I could provide him spiritual direction and hopefully bring him back to his senses and quite possibly back to his Catholic faith.

I met with the parents. They told me that they listened to me on Spanish Catholic radio, and they really begged me to intervene with their son. They told me they tried to bring a priest one time, but Andy cussed him out, began spitting at him, and threatened him with physical violence. The priest never came back; Andy was too dangerous and too unpredictable at this point.

I visited Andy in the hospital psychiatric ward at the request of his parents. Before I went, I had several conversations with him over the phone. When he was released from the hospital psychiatric ward, I visited him for several hours at his house. I went to Holy Mass that morning, prayed the holy Rosary, went to confession, and prayed prayers of protection over myself before I walked into the house to meet him. I also wore my St. Benedict medal and the Miraculous Medal around my neck. I sat down with Andy and spoke to him for hours; I prayed silently, binding the evil spirit from manifesting in my presence as I spoke to Andy.

I was getting to know Andy on a personal level, building bridges, catechizing, evangelizing, answering his questions, and giving him spiritual direction. He later told his parents, "There is something about Mr. Romero's presence that prevents me from cussing and swearing and going into a fit of rage and anger." I visited him about six more times, and when I prayed over him, every time, he would convulse, vibrate, and become dizzy, but he consented to be prayed over.

I did my best to give him spiritual direction, catechize, and evangelize him, but he was steeped in the occult, was confused and suicidal, and told me several times that this voice in his head tells him to kill his parents, then kill himself. The voice in his head would tell him that it would stop tormenting him and he would be at peace if he killed himself.

I would tell him, "You must resist those voices and pray through them till they go away."

He would listen, but he would tell me, "I can't fight this; I can't fight this. It's too strong for me; it's too strong for me."

I would pray over him for a long time, and he would tell me that my prayers would bring him temporary relief for a few hours but then the voice would come back in his head and the physical and mental torments would continue every night in his bedroom as soon as he turned off the lights. He was still adamant about *not* seeing a Catholic priest. His parents told me that I was the only adult that he respected and the only person around whom he didn't curse or who he wouldn't attack. They told me had a very evil side, what seemed to be a second personality, and that when that second personality would come forth, he would attack whoever was near: police, hospital personnel, his parents, anybody. He would speak in a language that neither his parents nor hospital personnel could understand and become very, very strong with a violent aversion to blessed holy objects.

Once I gained his trust (after our first meeting), he told me that something lived in his body; some spirit had entered his body two and a half years prior when he attended a satanic black mass. He said this spirit at first made him feel transcendent, like he was more powerful than anybody else. He said this spirit began tormenting him shortly after he gave his life to Satan at this satanic mass. The spirit began appearing to him every night as a hideous beast, dragon, snakes, or monster in his bedroom that would grab him from his bed by his ankles and throw him off his bed and against the wall, jump on him and smash him, and sometimes choke him.

His parents have heard voices and tussling coming from his bedroom as if two people were wrestling in there; yet Andy is an only child, there is nobody else in the house. Andy told me that the only way this evil spirit leaves him is when he turns on the lights in his room. He said he constantly hears voices in his head telling him, "Kill your parents, kill yourself, you're worthless, you're hopeless, you're a loser, end it all." He says these voices of negativity torment him every night like a bad recording. He says he can't sleep at night. That is why he sleeps throughout the day in between waking moments when he smokes marijuana, which calmed him down.

I told Andy quite clearly that only by returning to Jesus Christ and the Catholic Church would he be able to free himself from this demonic torment. He said he wasn't quite ready to return to the Catholic Church because he was wounded from being thrown out of Catholic school in the eighth grade for insubordination to the principal and a priest. He was also thrown out for smoking marijuana in the boy's bathroom back in 1995 (when it was still taboo).

He told me that he felt acute pain from the top of his head where he had the tattoo of Satan (a goats head inside a pentagram). He said he felt spirits entering his body and leaving his body from precisely the spot where he had the satanic tattoo. According to Fr. Amorth, "Some of the symbolism and designs (tattoos) on the body can make explicit or implicit referral to monsters or demons, nearly evoking them."[17] Jan Reagor, a lay Catholic involved in healing and deliverance ministry has discovered that demons can enter a person through demonic tattoos.[18] Demons are legalistic; they know when they have permission to inhabit the body of a person; they know when they have to leave. Living in mortal sin, having made a pact with Satan in a black mass, and having a satanic tattoo are the perfect storm for a demon to enter a person and torment them.

---

[17]   Gabriele Amorth, et al., *An Exorcist Explains the Demonic.*

[18]   Jan Reagor, "Taboo of Tattoos Is Seen in Cases Where Spirits May Have Attached to Them," *Spirit Daily*, www.spiritdaily.org/tattoospirits.htm.

I called Mundelein Seminary (the Pope Leo XIII Institute) and spoke to an exorcist (that I will leave unnamed per his request), and he told me that Andy must remove the satanic tattoo, go to confession, and then readily submit to deliverance and exorcism prayers at the hands of a trained Catholic priest in spiritual warfare. I told Andy's parents what must be done, and they said that they did not have the money to pay for a laser tattoo removal. My wife (Anita) took it upon herself to make an appointment for Andy to have the tattoo on his head removed, and she placed her credit card as payment. She figured that we were already committed to helping Andy, so we would just pay for the laser removal ourselves as an act of Christian charity for this destitute family whose son was being tormented by one or more demons.

Andy would text me every day and tell me that he was being tormented and tortured mentally and physically every day, and I would stop what I was doing and pray for him. He said it would go away temporarily when I would pray over him, and he would feel some relief for a few hours. My wife made an appointment for Andy on a Monday for the tattoo removal; it was Friday, and I told him to go to Church and just sit there and talk to God, but he said he wasn't ready to go just yet.

When his parents got home from work that afternoon, Andy went into a demonic anger fit, started punching holes in the walls and began breaking things in the house. He told his Dad and Mom, "Go outside right now, get out right now or I will kill you." He then tried to choke his father who managed to break free and run outside with his wife and close the door behind him. The parents ran to the front yard and stood on the sidewalk in front of their house. They were terrorized by their son.

The parents called my godson Salvador and asked him where I was. Salvador told them that I was speaking at a Church locally (in downtown Los Angeles). The parents told Salvador that Andy had become violent and explosive again, and he threw them out of the house. Salvador told them that he would drive over there and keep them company on the sidewalk in front of their house until Andy calmed down. Salvador arrived at the Mendoza's house in east LA and stood with them on the sidewalk in the front of the house. Salvador said the house was completely quiet. The Mendozas told him that Andy had stopped yelling and breaking things for about the last five minutes. Salvador told the Mendozas, "I'm going inside to talk to Andy."

The parents told him to be careful, as their son was unpredictable. Salvador went inside the house and began going from room to room calling out to Andy in a fairly loud voice. Salvador walked into the garage and saw Andy hanging by a rafter with a heavy-duty extension cord around his neck; he was still gurgling very softly and his face was pale. Salvador yelled to the parents for help. They ran in. Mrs. Mendoza fainted as she walked into the garage and saw her son hanging.

Salvador and Mr. Mendoza untied the cord from his neck and placed him on his back. Salvador (my godson) had trained for the last couple of summers as a junior lifeguard and began CPR while calling 911 immediately. Salvador continued until the paramedics arrived within about five minutes. As Salvador did CPR, he was also praying in his mind the Chaplet of the Divine Mercy for Andy. Salvador remembered a pamphlet I had given him awhile back which tells how Our Lord Jesus Christ promised St. Faustina (in 1931) that if you pray the Chaplet of the Divine Mercy in the presence of someone who is dying and that person receives the prayer with an open heart, the Lord promised that he will have mercy upon the dying person and save their soul.[19]

Salvador and the parents followed the paramedics to Los Angeles County Medical Center emergency. I was called, and I met the Mendozas there along with my wife. Andy was in the ICU, and his prognosis did not look good as he had gone too long without oxygen. He was breathing with a ventilator and was deathly still. He was in a coma.

His parents only allowed my godson, Salvador, myself, and my wife inside the room with Andy. We got on our knees and prayed the Chaplet of the Divine Mercy two feet away from him right in his ear. Then we prayed the Holy Rosary as well. We were all hoping he could hear us. Suddenly he turned his head in our direction and, with his eyes closed, acknowledged our prayer. I told Andy right in his ear, "It's time to open your heart to Jesus Christ; he loves you. Open your heart, receive him, and ask him for his love and forgiveness. Don't wait; it's time to give Jesus your heart right now!"

The doctor told me that even though he was in a coma, he could hear every word. I called a Catholic priest that was

---

[19]   Maria Faustina Kowalska, *Diary of Saint Maria Faustina Kowalska: Divine Mercy in My Soul* (Marian Press, 2016), 811, 835, 1015.

in the hospital making visits, and I brought him in to the room to give Andy the sacrament of the Anointing of the Sick. This was not a coincidence; it was a God-incidence. We (my wife, my godson, and me) came back the next day Tuesday, Wednesday, and Thursday and prayed the Chaplet and Rosary. I whispered into his ear every day, "Jesus loves you. Our Lady is here to protect you. Open your heart to them now, and ask Jesus for his mercy. Invite him into your heart." The doctor said he never moved except when we would come in to pray; he would move his head in the direction where we stood praying for him.

Andy died of a massive heart attack that Friday in the early morning hours. My heart was in pain seeing his parents' deep anguish and sadness at this whole tragedy of a young life cut down by way of suicide as a result of drug addiction and satanic involvement. The Catholic Church services were done very discreetly; only the parents, my wife, my godson, and I attended. It was "a time to weep" (Eccl 3:1–4). We prayed a Rosary novena at the Mendozas house, and I prayed a Chaplet of Divine Mercy novena on my own. I can't even imagine how it must feel to bury your son, but Our Lady does.

Life continues for all of us. This tragedy made the Mendozas become practicing Catholics. They convalidated their marriage in the Catholic Church after cohabitating for twenty years. About three months after their son Andy died, I received a phone call from Mr. Mendoza at about 3 a.m. He was exhilarated and very emotional; he spoke fast, like he was electrically charged. He said, "Jesse, Andy appeared to us; he appeared to us in our bedroom at the foot of our bed.

My wife saw him also." I told him calm down, slow down, speak slowly. Mr. Mendoza said his son appeared to him like a ghost at the foot of his bed in the bedroom and was shouting and pleading to him, saying, "Daddy, Daddy, help me. I'm burning here, help me. I'm burning here. I'm burning. Please, Daddy, go and offer thirty Masses for me. Please, Daddy, go and offer thirty Masses for me." His son then disappeared. Mrs. Mendoza was also on the phone with me; she confirmed that she saw the exact same vision of her son that Mr. Mendoza saw. Mr. Mendoza, who was very choked up, asked me, "Jesse, what does this mean?"

Mr. Mendoza was a very simple low information Catholic, and his son knew virtually nothing about the Catholic faith in his short life on earth. I told Mr. Mendoza, "Praise the Lord. Based on the vision of your son, he is in purgatory. There is a pious Catholic tradition given to us by Pope Gregory the Great in AD 590 that if you offer thirty consecutive Masses for the soul of someone who dies in a state of grace (i.e., with no mortal sins), the Lord will set them free from purgatory and they will enter heaven on the thirtieth Mass. Mr. Mendoza went in the morning to offer thirty consecutive Mass for the repose of the soul of his son Andy at his parish.

This young man was like St. Dismas, the good thief who stole heaven right before he died because he was forgiven by God himself. Objectively speaking, Andy's story is a modern-day tragedy; he committed suicide at a very young age, was a Satanist, and a drug addict. He made a pact with Satan and even had a satanic tattoo on the top of his head as a sign of his commitment to Satan. By all outward appearances, Andy was clearly headed for hell, but at the last moment of his life, it appears very strongly that he opened his heart to Christ while in a coma, received the prayers, repented in his heart and had contrition. It appears as if he totally opened himself to the sanctifying grace of the sacrament of the Anointing of the Sick and died at peace and friendship with God. It appears that he did, in fact, have his many sins forgiven through the sacrament of the Anointing of the Sick and was being purified by the fires of God's love in purgatory. Mr. Mendoza's vision of his son is evidence that Andy was saved like the thief on the cross in the last moments of his life. My hope is that Andy has been released from purgatory and is now in heaven praying for us. My hope is that I will see him one day, no longer with a satanic tattoo on his head, but washed and made totally clean by the blood of the lamb.

What was the point of entry? The point of entry occurred when he invited the diabolical into his life at the satanic black mass, and the diabolical remained with him because he lived in a perpetual state of mortal sin. Demons are attracted to evil people who live in mortal sin. This is known as "the law of attraction."

Our Lady Smashes a Demon—Fifth Encounter

There was a lady named Lola that called the east LA sheriff station to report a burglary in her apartment in the Maravilla housing projects. I was dispatched to answer the call and take a report of the crime. I arrived, made contact with Lola, and took down the information; she looked very despondent and depressed, as if she had not slept for days. She told me,

"Deputy, I have a bigger problem than this burglary that I am reporting. Someone is trying to kill me." I contacted the station dispatcher and stated that I would be there awhile taking another criminal complaint. I gave her my undivided attention, and she told me the following.

She said that when she was young, her father consecrated her to the devil in a satanic ritual. Her mother had her baptized as an infant in the Catholic Church, but her father suppressed the practice of the Catholic faith in the family. Her mother would try to sneak off to Mass and pray the Rosary in the closet, but her father would beat his wife if and when he caught her practicing her faith. She said her father was "a monster." And she told me in detail the many horrible things that she was forced to do in the cult of Satan that her father would take her to.

She was involved in forced sexual orgies, animal sacrifice, human sacrifice, constant drug use and intoxication, hexes, curses, incantations, spells, drinking animal and human blood as well as urine, grave desecration, vandalizing Catholic churches, destroying sacred holy objects, and stealing and desecrating the Holy Eucharist by going to Mass, receiving communion in the hand, and bringing the Sacred Host to her Father for desecration.

Lola told me vividly how she, as a child, would be taken to the desert every summer for a week. A satanic priest would give them lectures on discipleship around a campfire. According to Lola, he would then, before their very eyes, change into a black wolf and start running around them to display his occult power and put fear into them. The wolf would than transform back into a man and continue his satanic lecture. Believe it or not as is your right; that is what Lola told me.

She saw this every summer from about the age of ten to eighteen. Everything she was told to do, she did by force and compulsion. If she didn't, the satanic members would beat her mercilessly and torture her. Lola told me that when she was eighteen, her mother left her father. Lola went with her mother and joined the Catholic Church in Guadalajara (by her own free will). Finally, her mother and Lola were able to practice their Catholic faith without the menacing threats of her father who did not know where they lived and went on to commit suicide. Lola went through RCIA at nineteen. Lola told me that she knew the Catholic faith was the true religion from God because she was told this, ironically enough, by her satanic elders. Lola also said she was told by the satanic leaders (while being forced to practice Satanism):

- The Catholic Church was considered the enemy because it alone was founded by Jesus Christ.
- Satanists mock the Catholic Mass during their worship of Satan, which they call the "black mass."
- Satanists have a satanic rosary.
- Satanists are compelled to steal the Holy Eucharist and bring it to their satanic black mass for desecration because Satanists believe in the "real presence of Christ" in the Holy Eucharist.
- Satanists don't mock or try to imitate protestants, Jewish, or Muslim worship services because they have no power.
- Satanists try to find out the identity of the diocesan exorcist in order to barrage him with continual hexes,

curses, and spells. (Incidentally, this is why most exorcists wish to remain anonymous.)

Shortly after RCIA, her pastor in Mexico referred her to the diocesan exorcist. She told me that she had received about two dozen exorcisms from the age of nineteen to about twenty-nine in Guadalajara and Mexico City by the respective diocesan exorcists. She journaled the dates of each exorcism and showed it to me. She and her mother moved back to the United States because her satanic sect found out where they lived and began harassing them.

Lola was twenty-nine when she moved to the Maravilla housing projects in east LA with her mother, who was in her early fifties. Lola was in her early thirties when I met her. She told me an evil spirit had come back to torment her; she also admitted that she was not practicing her Catholic faith as fervently as she did when she lived in Mexico. She asked me if I knew a Catholic priest who could continue treating her for her diabolical vexation and torment. I told her that I did and sent her to the priest at an area church. I told her to sign up there as a parishioner because she was just bouncing around from one Catholic Church to another without making any commitment to a parish.

She did as I told her and became a parishioner there. The priest, who was adept at healing and spiritual warfare, began treating Lola for all the emotional baggage and woundedness that she carried from being a former Satanist. He had several prayer sessions over Lola with his deliverance team which lasted about a year. One day, I was taking a person that I had arrested in handcuffs to that same church. My prisoner was

Catholic, so I was going to take him to the church and invite him to pray in front of the Blessed Sacrament before I took him to jail for his crime (a practice that I did on occasion when I felt the Holy Spirit leading me to do so).

The priest was in the church about to hear confessions, but as soon as he saw me, he came up to me and asked me if I could help him pray over Lola that coming Monday at 9 p.m. inside the church. He told me that I made a lasting impression on her a year ago when I went to her apartment and took a burglary report. He also told me that he knew my parents well and my parents had helped him on several occasions with healing and deliverance sessions over victims of diabolical torment. He jokingly told me that I had to continue the tradition of my parents. I agreed to help Father; truth be told, I was honored to be asked by such a well-known spiritual warfare priest in East Los Angeles. I told him that I would be honored to help him assist in this healing and deliverance session that he was going to have with Lola.

He told me to bring my wife, as the sacrament of marriage is very powerful during intercessory prayer. My wife and I prepared for nine days straight prior to the session: we went to confession a week before the prayer session, prayed the daily Rosary and divine mercy for nine days, fasted the day of the prayer session, and went to Holy Mass that morning in preparation to assist the priest as he prayed over Lola. He had consulted with the priest exorcist from Mexico that had been treating Lola; that priest had certified that Lola had all the signs of possession, which are:

1. a sudden capacity to speak unknown languages,
2. abnormal physical strength,
3. the ability to disclose hidden occurrences or events,
4. and a vehement aversion to God, the litany to the Virgin Mary, the litany of the saints, and religious images, especially the cross.

Monday night came, and we drove to the church. Lola was there with her mother and three brothers. I was there with my wife (who was assisting as an intercessor and as a witness lest any one of us be accused of sexual improprieties). My wife and I prayed the Holy Rosary, the Divine Mercy, and the Angelus on our way to the Church. We met with the priest. Lola and her family arrived about thirty minutes after us. Father was filling us in on her case.

She had been ritually consecrated by her father in Mexico as a child, and her father brought her up worshipping La Santa Muerte, while her mother tried to bring her up in the Catholic faith behind her husband's back. Lola was poorly formed in Catholicism (by her own admission) as a result of her involvement with the cult of Santa Muerte (literally "Holy" or "Saint" Death, but in actuality a vehicle through which Satan has entered the lives of many Hispanic Catholics) throughout the course of her life up until she was eighteen.

As mentioned above, her father committed suicide and her mother watched over Lola, but she was damaged goods at this point. She had been involved in so many satanic rituals that she had opened the doors of her soul to the diabolical. Lola arrived at the church; she was completely cooperative with the healing and deliverance session. She seemed like a simple pious young lady who was living out her Catholic faith to the best of her ability between episodes of being tormented by evil spirits. She told Father that she had just gone to Sunday Mass the night before and she had also gone to confession two days before.

A chair was placed in front of the altar in the sanctuary for Lola; one of her brothers brought a small workout mat. I looked at him kind of surprised, and he told me, "Trust me, we're going to need it." The three brothers said that when the demon manifests, it takes over her body and she goes into a violent rage and becomes very strong. Her mother and my wife were behind her as prayer intercessors and as witnesses. The priest said a prayer of protection over all of us who were going to assist him as intercessors. Lola sat down on a chair with her eyes closed. Father placed his stole on and exposed Jesus Christ in the Blessed Sacrament on the altar fifteen feet in front of Lola. As soon as she looked at the Blessed Sacrament, Lola started having demonic manifestations.

- Her body expanded like a puffer fish.
- Her arms and legs became as hard as wood.
- She thrashed and threw punches at us. The priest was punched in the jaw and pushed very hard; he fell back about ten feet, sliding on his buttocks, and hit the back of his head on the side altar rail.
- She was grabbing our sacramentals around our necks and rosaries and trying to rip them off. Father sprayed her hands with holy water and she would let go immediately. She would jerk her hands away and scream when she was

sprayed with holy water as if she was being burned.

- Her eyes raged with anger; they looked pitch black, neither pupil nor iris were visible.

- She began speaking in different languages. It sounded like gibberish. She pointed to one of her brothers and disclosed some hidden embarrassing unconfessed sins about her brother's lifestyle. This brother was so humiliated that he just stood there petrified and did not help in prayer or in holding her down.

- She snorted, grunted like an animal, growled like a dog, laughed (like Vincent Price), and spoke like Smeagol from the *Lord of the Rings*.

- She broke free from all of our grips and she grabbed me by the shirt (chest area) and flung me to the wall. My wife said I was airborne with my body in an L position. I hit the Church wall with my back, and there was a boom. I got back up and grabbed her wrist to help her brothers hold her down. Before the session began, the priest had prayed a prayer of protection for all of us, and he told us, "God will protect you tonight, nobody will be hurt." The only thing that was hurt was my ego: that a petite short woman (weighing about 120 pounds) could toss me, an over two-hundred-pound former kickboxing champion, like a ball.

- Lola was on her stomach, and her two brothers and her mother and I were holding her down. Remember, one brother was petrified (because his sins were exposed out loud), so the mother came in to take his place. I held Lola's right wrist down with both of my arms. I was in a pushup position using all my strength; her arm was as hard as wood. Suddenly, as I was looking at her right arm that I was holding down, I saw three deep scratches appear on the back of her right arm, and they started bleeding.

- Lola started calling someone with her index fingers. The priest said that she was calling demons. Suddenly every single door in the Church was being pounded hard by someone outside, yet nobody was out there. The parking lot was locked; it was 11 p.m.—there was nobody out there. Father sprayed her fingers with holy water, and she curled her fingers into a fist and the doors stopped pounding. Father later told us that it was demons pounding the doors, trying to distract and scare us so that we would stop praying.

The priest had the book *Manual of Minor Exorcisms* along with his Bible, and he prayed the most relevant prayers from those books. He would go from spontaneous prayers to litanies to deprecative prayers to imperative prayers to Latin chants. It was like watching a physician perform surgery, as Father was very tactical in his prayers. Lola fought and struggled with us for three hours. We were all exhausted. Lola's mother asked, "Padre, que vamos hacer ahora?" (Father, what are we going to do right now?)

The only prayer I hadn't heard prayed at that point in three hours of struggling with the demonized woman was the holy Rosary. Father said, "Pray to Mary, pray to Mary!" We all started praying the Hail Mary, and Lola screamed in pain. It sounded like we dropped a microphone into hell. We prayed in English and Spanish, but it had little effect on her. Father started praying the Hail Mary in Latin, and Lola started screaming as if she were being tortured. She started yelling (in another scratchy voice that was not hers), "Get her off me, get her off me."

Father said, "In Jesus name, tell me who is on you?"

She said, "The woman, the woman, get her off me."

The priest told us, "Don't stop praying; we found out what it doesn't like."

My wife looked up and said, "Our Lady is here, Our Lady is here." We kept praying the Rosary while Father prayed the Hail Mary in Latin. The priest's prayers in Latin seemed to cause the evil spirit in Lola more trauma. She kept yelling (the voice was not hers) as if she were in excruciating pain, and then went flat on her stomach in a cruciform position. Her body began getting long as if something was on top of her and smashing her like a pancake. I rubbed both of my eyes with my fist and made sure that I was not hallucinating, but my wife verified that she saw the same thing on the drive home.

Lola's body returned to its regular size like an accordion, and she than began to convulse for about thirty seconds. Father said that the demons were leaving. Lola let out a sigh of relief and rested on her stomach and closed her eyes for about a minute; she sounded physically exhausted. Father and her mother sat her up, and Lola said, "They left; they didn't like that last prayer. What language was that?" He said, "It was the Hail Mary in Latin." She said, "Can I please have Holy Communion?" and Father gave her the sacrament.

So, what was the point of entry through which the diabolical entered this woman? Lola was consecrated to Satan as a child by an evil father through no fault of her own. Fr. Amorth, one of the world's preeminent exorcists before he passed away, wrote, "Curses invoke evil, and the origin of all evil is demonic. When curses are spoken with true perfidy, especially if there is a blood relationship between the one who casts them and the accursed, the outcome can be terrible." Fr. Amorth stresses the fact that there are incredibly strong bonds between family members and that curses that operate within these familial bonds can have terrible consequences. He gives several examples of cases he worked: a young man cursed by his own father at birth, parents cursing their daughter-in-law at their wedding, and a man whose grandmother cursed a photograph of him, resulting in ill legs and multiple surgeries.[20]

Radio Studio—Sixth Encounter

I drove to El Monte, California, to attend a meeting at a Spanish Catholic Radio Apostolate since I was a radio talk show host on that network. The meeting was relative to the upcoming pledge drive and radiothon. I arrived about an hour early and figured that I would just do a holy hour in the chapel before the meeting. As I walked toward the chapel in the courtyard, I saw about six of the female employees surrounding a woman who was sitting on a stone bench that was about ten feet long. The ladies were praying the Rosary in a loud manner, and I immediately sensed that they were

---

[20]   "Fr. Amorth on the 4 Types of Curses." *St. Peter's List*, May 14, 2017, stpeterslist.com/amorth-and-curses.

dealing with an individual who had some type of demonic vexation.

I looked at the woman—she was Hispanic and in her mid-thirties—and she was making guttural noises as if she were gargling water. She had slight frothing of the mouth, and her head was moving side to side very rapidly. I didn't think it was possible to move your head side to side that fast, and her long hair was flopping quickly from side to side so that it looked like someone was shaking a mop. What was most bizarre was that she was sliding on the bench on her buttocks from one end to the other end and back again, but her feet were not moving, and her hands were folded over her stomach. Her feet were just sliding, yet she was not using her feet at all. The Catholic prayer warrior ladies were happy to see me. I asked them, "Where's Father?"

One of them told me that he saw this woman having demonic manifestations, and he ran away and locked himself in his office. While running away he said, "Take care of it yourself. Jesse is coming; he will help you."

I wondered why this priest would run from this confrontation. He was a highly educated priest with a PhD in dogmatic theology from the Angelicum, a Pontifical University in Rome. I just scratched my head, but I put that aside and immediately jumped into the circle of prayer and began assisting the ladies in praying for this demonized lady.

One of the ladies told me that she came to the Catholic radio ministry center to get some help because she was tired of being attacked by this evil spirit. As the ladies prayed the Rosary, I began to pray deliverance prayers as well: the Our Father, St. Michael the Archangel prayer, the Soul of Christ prayer, and the St. Benedict prayer. I told one of the ladies to bring me some holy water and a large crucifix. She came back with these sacramentals and gave them to me. I began dousing her with holy water and praying spontaneous prayers of healing, renunciation, and deliverance. She stopped sliding and remained motionless, and she stopped shaking her head like a shark with prey in its mouth. I told her to gaze upon the crucifix and repeat with me, "Jesus, I trust in you! Jesus, I trust in you!" She snapped out of her trance, and her eyes, which were rolled back (no pupil or iris present; they were pure white), came back to normal.

I told her to follow me to the front office as all the ladies surrounded her and kept praying the holy Rosary. The victim followed me as well and kept repeating, "Jesus, I trust in you!" (in Spanish). You could tell she wanted to get healed and set free from the diabolical; she was totally cooperative with us. I kept praying healing and deliverance prayers as well as I escorted her to the front office. When we all entered the front office, I gave her a cup of water and one of the other ladies wiped the saliva that dripped from the ends of her mouth, and another lady started combing her hair. We were trying to show her Christian charity, which is a powerful weapon against the diabolical.

Suddenly, she started screaming and said (in Spanish), "There it is, there it is!" as she pointed to the corner of the office. She said, "Can't you see it; it came back to get me!" She looked completely terrified, so we all began praying again over her; the ladies started praying the holy Rosary, and I started praying deliverance prayers over her in Latin. She threw herself (or was thrown to the wall) on her back very hard and slid down the wall onto the floor on her back. I continued dousing her with holy water, praying deliverance prayers in Latin; she went limp and closed her eyes as if she were unconscious.

We kept praying over her, and after two or three minutes, she opened her eyes. We helped her sit on a chair and she said (in Spanish), "It left me; it didn't like your prayers." She was referring to the deliverance prayers in Latin. The ladies took charge of her; they were going to take her down the street to a Catholic Church so that she could go to confession. The ladies were loving her and catechizing her when I left. About a year after this incident, the priest that ran away when he saw this demonized woman was transferred to Mexico because of sexual accusations with a woman from the radio ministry. Then it made sense to me why he ran away when he saw this demonized woman; most likely, he was in mortal sin and his prayers would have been weak and ineffective, to say the least.

What was the point of entry for this woman? She admitted to us that she had been practicing witchcraft for many years, and she was tired of being part of the occult. She felt a strong desire to be set free and return to the practice of her Catholic faith.

Three O'clock Encounter in Fresno—Seventh Encounter

I was invited to speak at a parish mission in Fresno, California, at St. Mary's Church in May of 2000 (the Jubilee Year). A married couple picked me up at the airport, Rick and Sally Doe. They were part of the committee that sponsored the

Evangelization Conference that I was giving at the parish. This couple and I hit it off right away. They took me to their house, which was large and beautiful. We had dinner before the conference at their house on Friday night, and they made me feel very comfortable. We drove to the parish, I gave talks there, packed up my products, and left for the hotel. Rick and Sally begged me to stay at their house. Their "nest" was empty and they had a huge house with several empty bedrooms. I agreed, so we canceled my hotel reservation and off to their house we went.

They had three young adult children who were all in college, so the house was fairly empty. Rick was so happy that I was there. While we were talking, he and his wife were drinking wine; I was drinking hot tea because I had to preach the next day so I was soothing my throat. It was about midnight when they finally showed me to my room, and we called it an evening. I went to bed and closed the door to the room, but I did not lock it. There was a digital clock right next to me; I set the alarm clock for 7 a.m., did my night prayers, and went to sleep.

A few hours later while I was in deep sleep, the door to the room flew open and hit the wall hard. Rick (the homeowner) came running into the room and yelling, "Jesse help me, help me; the devil's in my room. Help me, help me!" I was startled and jumped out of my bed instinctively in a martial art combat stance. I looked at the digital clock and it was 3 a.m. (the preferred hour for Satanists and witches). I put my pants on and followed Rick to his bedroom; his face was white and he was crying, petrified with fear. We entered his room and he jumped back into his bed. Rick and Sally covered themselves with their blankets right underneath their noses. They were both in full panic and screaming, "Help Jesse, help us Jesse. There he is; he's in the corner. He's laughing at us. Help us." I took a martial arts combative stance (as if that would scare a demon). I did it more for me so that I would muster up courage and take appropriate action. I felt an evil presence in the room. I began praying spontaneous prayers, deliverance prayers, the Rosary, and the Divine Mercy chaplet over and over again. Rick and Sally kept pointing to different parts of the room and saying, "He's over there. Help us. Now he's over there; now he's over there." Each time they would point to where this demon was in the room, I quickly faced that way in a karate stance and directed my prayers in that direction.

This went on for about thirty to forty minutes. I felt like a bullfighter in a bullfight, but I could not see my enemy. I prayed from the depths of my heart because I was afraid. This couple was dead serious. They were seeing something in their bedroom that was tormenting them. After about forty minutes of me jumping around the room in a karate stance and praying from my heart, Sally said, "He left; he left. He's gone." Rick and Sally hugged each other and were both in tears. Rick said, "Thank you, Jesse; thank you so much. He left the room. He's gone." I prayed an Our Father, three Hail Marys, and a Glory Be with them to bring them comfort and closure. I walked back to the guest room where I was sleeping. This time, I locked the door.

I laid down and could not sleep the rest of the night. I just stared at the roof in semi shock at what had just happened.

What was the point of entry? Unknown, and we did not discuss the incident the next day. I went to the church the next day, preached a few conferences, drove to the airport, and flew home.

A Cold Wind Enters the Hall—Eighth Encounter

I was giving an evangelization retreat at my former parish—Guardian Angel Church in Pacoima, California—one Saturday. I was assisted by my wife and a team I had put together of very faithful committed Catholics. It was a Saturday afternoon, and there were about fifty attendees in the hall along with about twelve retreat team members. I was presenting a talk called "Spiritual Warfare, put on the Catholic Armor of God." I was told by one of the retreat attendees, Robert Solano (from the Brotherhood of St. Dismas, Orange County chapter), that one of the ladies that was attending named Lupita had a long history of dabbling in the occult (Santa Muerte and witchcraft).

I noticed throughout the retreat that Lupita looked melancholy, depressed, and seemed to be in physical pain at times. I introduced myself to her and welcomed her to this evangelization retreat. I wanted her to feel comfortable because I was now aware of her dark past. I sat in front of her and opened my Holy Bible to Psalm 91 and placed it on her hands which she had on her lap. I told her to please read Psalm 91, which is a Jewish exorcism prayer. She began vibrating, grimacing in pain, and bouncing the Holy Bible in her hands like it was hot coals. I took the Holy Bible back into my hands, and she immediately stopped all her physical manifestations. In my mind I said, "Oh no, we're going to have problems with her. Lord come to my assistance, heal her, and set her free."

The retreat continued, and on Saturday night during my "Spiritual Warfare" presentation, I talked about the dangers of Satanism and explained and defined demonic possession, obsession, oppression, infestation, temptation, witchcraft, spells, and curses. Lupita stood up during my presentation and gently disrupted me and said, "Everything he is saying is true. It's true, I know, it's all happened to me." Then she held up a rosary that she had in her pocket that was broken in pieces. Everybody in the room sensed the presence of evil at that moment; I sure did. There was a long silence. I told Lupita, "Thank you for affirming my presentation through your personal experience. I would like to talk with you more about it later on."

Lupita sat down, and I wrapped up my presentation shortly thereafter. I ended with a long prayer of healing and deliverance where I asked the attendees to repent, renounce any evil attachments in their past, and open their heart right now to Our Lord and Savior Jesus Christ and consecrate themselves to him. During this prayer, I saw Lupita start shaking uncontrollably in her chair. She spoke gibberish and her head was turning left and right very quickly.

I left the podium and a friend, Hector Barragan, walked up on the stage and began leading the Rosary because all the other retreat attendees were frightened. Some of them were so afraid at what they saw that they just ran out of the hall. Suddenly, the temperature dropped in the hall as a cold wind came in that was not there before (everybody noticed it because we all talked about this later). My wife and I and a few retreat team members escorted Lupita behind the stage to a room where her demonic manifestations continued very strongly. She was in a trance, her eyes rolled to the back of her head and they were completely white—no pupil, no iris present—and she vibrated like a generator. A second evil personality had taken over her body and voice.

We laid her on a couch, and she yelled in a man's voice, "I am Satan," at the top of her lungs. Her body than morphed into a U position on the couch. Her feet were on the couch, her stomach was arched up, and her hands were flat on the couch. She was screaming in pain; it was as if some invisible force was just bending her in half like a gumby toy. What came out of her voice for the next thirty minutes (at least) sounded like someone dropped a microphone in hell. Everybody in the room was on their knees praying the Rosary without missing a beat. My wife and I started doing these special deliverance prayers called Auxilium Christianorum prayers, which were written by a team of Catholic exorcists. Auxilium Christianorum means "help of Christians," which is a title of the Blessed Virgin Mary. These are lay-approved deliverance prayers that call upon the intercession of Our Lady to deliver a person from the diabolical. (I have these prayers on page 117 of my prayer book *Lord Prepare my Hands for Battle*. Or you can get them on the internet at Auxiliumchristianorum.org.)

We saturated Lupita with a battering ram of prayers. All of us were on our knees except me, my wife, and Eddie Chavez. We were making sure that Lupita did not hit her head during this demonic physical torture that she was experiencing. After about thirty minutes, she let out a scream and her eyes opened like a saucer. Her pupils and iris returned, and she was seeing something. In sheer terror, she said, "He's in the corner; he's in the corner. He's leaving; he's leaving. He's flying. He went out the window!" All her demonic manifestations ceased, her body fell flat on the couch in a supine position, and my wife began caressing her hand and forehead as we continued to pray the Rosary for the next few minutes. She told us that she saw an evil spirit leave her body. She said it was very, very physically painful when it left her. We took her to our pastor so that she could receive the sacrament of confession, which is "a hundred times more powerful than an exorcism."

What was the point of entry for Lupita? She had invited demons into her life through the Santa Muerte cult and witchcraft. This is known as the law of invitation. She wanted to return to the practice of her Catholic faith, and that was why she was getting attacked by the diabolical. She had invited this demon through practicing the occult. The demon was tormenting her because she was not fully evangelized or catechized (she had a very shallow understanding of her faith). She said that her network of witch friends had put curses on her because they knew she was trying to come back to the Catholic Church. You are powerless against curses when you are not living in a state of grace.

Another Cold Wind Enters the Parish Hall—Ninth Encounter

It was yet another Saturday afternoon at Guardian Angel Catholic Church in Pacoima, and we (Team Jesus) were giving yet another evangelization retreat. A thirty-something Hispanic lady named Maria told me that she was just returning to the Catholic Church after a long hiatus. She also told me that she had been involved in the occult for the last fifteen years and had been very unchaste in her past. She told me that she was living with a married man and that she had been a nude dancer at a "gentleman's club" (what an oxymoron since there are no gentlemen there). She quit her job after several years of working there because the manager made them all become intoxicated with illegal narcotics before they went on stage and performed naked.

Maria said she was consistently intoxicated every day for about five years; that was the only way she could perform and dance naked in front of men. As a result of this, she was addicted to cocaine and meth for years, but she had now resolved to change her life and come back to the Catholic Church and give God a chance. She was a simple soul who had been extremely emotionally wounded by her past poor choices.

I asked her why she quit her job. She said that she quit because on the last night she was there dancing naked for the nasty men, she saw everybody's face in the club turn into an evil diabolical face; she had seen this before, but on this particular night, as she looked at their feet, everybody there had goat hooves instead of feet coming out of their pants.

Maria became so frightened at seeing all the men in the audience turn into demons that she ran off the stage, put on her clothes, ran to her car, and drove home extremely terrified. A good Catholic neighbor who had been trying to evangelize her invited her to this evangelization retreat that

I was giving. Maria decided to give God a try, so she came. Maria fit right in with the rest of the retreatants, broken men and woman (that we all are) coming to be healed and comforted by Our Lord Jesus Christ.

During my presentation on "Spiritual Warfare – Put on the Armor of God," Maria started speaking out of turn very loudly. She said, "Jesse, Jesse help me. It's burning; it's inside of me. Get him out; get him out. Help me; help me, Jesse." Maria was in the front row. She did not fall off the chair; she slid off the chair like a snake and lay on her back and moved like a snake, her eyes rolled back—there was no pupil, no iris—she was in a demonic trance. My wife, Eddie Chavez, and I ran over to assist her while Hector Barragan (another Team Jesus retreat team member) calmed everybody down and led the attendees in praying the holy Rosary. It was time to storm heaven (and hell for that matter) with prayer.

Once again, a cold chill entered the hall, and some retreat attendees were so afraid that they ran out. Maria was on her back, screaming, "Help me, help me. It burns; it burns. Get him out of my stomach; get him out; please get him out. It's hurting me." We saw her stomach rising up and then going back down like "whack-a-moles" at a carnival. Her stomach would rise in different areas and then go back down. It reminded me of the movie *Alien* where this space alien came out of the protagonist's stomach. Maria's body looked as if you put a snake and a mongoose inside a potato sack and let them fight. That's the best way to describe what we saw.

We carried her to the outside patio because her actions were very frightening to the attendees, many of whom were neophytes, pew-warming Sunday Catholics simply trying to grow deeper in their faith. The retreatants were praying the Rosary inside the hall. I ran to the sacristy to call my pastor who was about to process in to celebrate Holy Mass. He looked at me and said, "You know what to do!" He then blessed me and said, "Go with my blessing and don't be afraid, I will offer this Mass for her." I ran back to the hall (which was connected to the sacristy), and we started praying over Maria with the Auxilium Christianorum prayers.

We prayed fervently for Maria for about thirty to forty minutes nonstop, all while the demonic manifestations continued and looked like epileptic seizures and convulsion. Her stomach continued rising in different parts as if something were trying to get out. We were covering her with prayer. The physical manifestations finally stopped in her body, and she laid still. She woke up out of the trance and said, "It left. Thank you, thank you. It left. How can I ever thank you?" She cried tears of joy. We sat her up, had her drink holy water, and we gave her a blessed rosary to put around her neck. Another retreat team member went to go call the pastor who was finishing the celebration of Holy Mass so that he could come and hear her confession and give her absolution. Meanwhile, I took her to the corner of a room behind the stage. I loaned her a big crucifix and told her to be silent before the crucifix for ten minutes and tell Jesus how much she loves him and needs him. I also told her to then say the St. Dismas prayer ten times: "Jesus, remember me when you come into your kingdom" (cf. Lk 23:42).

What was the point of entry? Maria had invited demons into her life through drug addiction, sexual immorality, and living in an unrepentant state of mortal sin. She wanted to return to the practice of her Catholic faith; that was why she was getting attacked by the diabolical. An evil spirit had attached to her as a result of her living a sinful lifestyle. (Remember, demons are attracted to people that live in unrepentant, unconfessed mortal sin.) Maria was not fully evangelized or catechized, so she was a prime target for demonic vexation. She said that she had also consulted witches to put curses on her enemies. The demons were coming after Maria because they knew she was trying to come back to the Catholic Church.

* * *

I just gave you, the reader, nine cases in which I encountered the diabolical. Stories like these are important to share because they point to the reality of the devil and his minions who seek to drag us all down to hell. However, it is also important to know some important facts about our adversary and possession. I give you the following information for your need-to-know file.

> There are two principal types of demons that cause two distinct types of possession—the *clausi* and the *aperti*. A *clausus* demon causes the possessed to close his eyes (with them rolled back) when entering into a trance. An *apertus* demon causes the possessed to keep his eyes open while in a trance, giving looks of anger and rage, and speaking a great deal. The *aperti* are loquacious and violent, and the possessed person often needs to be held down during the exorcism; the *clausi*

will speak after some time of prayer, always without opening their eyes, but others are completely mute.[21]

The *abditi* (latin for *hidden* or *secret*) demons are those that hide in the interior of the possessed person without showing themselves in any way. The person notices a change in his life and feels strange things that make him suspect there is an external force that has entered him. He can even experience preternatural phenomena. But when the priest prays, the demon resists and gives no sign of being present. . . . In some cases, *abditi* demons have been able to resist two hours of exorcism without giving the least sign of their presence. After much insistence, though, the demon cannot resist any longer and shows himself in all his rage and with all the signs that often appear in possession. . . . The *abditi* demons . . . are not . . . a distinct type of demon; they are simply demons who hide themselves within the person. Once they have been forced to reveal themselves, they will act like the *clausi* or *aperti* demons.[22]

---

[21] José Antonio Fortea, *Interview with an Exorcist: an Insiders Look at the Devil, Demonic Possession, and the Path to Deliverance* (Ascension Press, 2006).

[22] Ibid., 77, 88.

Encounters With Witches

First Encounter With a Witch

When I was around sixteen years old, there was a lady in my neighborhood who was infatuated with me. She was ten years older than me and divorced. I met her at a street party, and for her, it was love at first sight. It was flattering to my ego, but I was sixteen and so immature in all respects. She asked for my number and she would call my house incessantly. She would drive by my house (I lived with my parents) about four or five times a day. She would leave love letters in the mailbox. I met her through her sister, who was my age and attended San Fernando High School with me. She told me that her older sister was in love with me; I certainly did not understand what love meant at sixteen years old. Certainly not Christian love known as agape, which means unconditional love, total self-donation, self-sacrificing love. That definition was nowhere on my radar.

To be honest, even though I was young, I was turned off by this older lady because she had a reputation for being promiscuous according to some of my friends in high school who had attended parties with her. Even though I was young, I could see that this lady had been extremely wounded by men in her past relationships. She hounded me for about three months, so one day, out of pity and peer pressure, I went to have lunch with her at a fast-food place at the San Fernando mall.

We started seeing each other, and she saw that I was not experienced or promiscuous, so she took me to a "healer." She said that the healer would help me fall in love with her and be with her forever. I started to understand that this woman was impulsive and irrational. We drove over to this "botanica." (A botanica is a storefront where occult items are sold and often there is a back room or parlor where occult activity and witchcraft occurs for paying customers.)

Immediately, God's grace kicked in, and I knew that this botanica in San Fernando where I found myself was actually the parlor of a witch and that I was flirting with evil. I sat there very nervous with this older woman, and she said, "Don't be afraid; it will not hurt at all." The older Hispanic lady introduced herself as hermana curandera Gloria (sister Gloria the healer).

I felt very uncomfortable with this witch in front of me lighting candles and incense around the parlor; she had a lot of masks that looked like demons plastered all over the wall; she had a lot of Aztec pagan images and statues. She also had a statue of Our Lady of Guadalupe in the corner of the room which was illuminated with six black candles around her. Seven is the number of God, the number of perfection, the number of the covenant. Six is the number of imperfection; add two more sixes and you have 666, the number of the beast (cf. Rv 13:18).

The older lady that was in love with me looked very comfortable, like she had been here many times before. I thought to myself that I was not the first guy she had brought here to have a "love spell" put on him. The witch brought some cards to the table where I was sitting. The lights were dim. She took out an egg and started reciting some incantations in a language that was not Spanish or English. She had an egg in one hand as she made a circular motion over my head;

she grabbed my hand with her other hand and stared at it as if she were reading something on my palm. At that point, I was spooked, and the Holy Spirit that I had received at baptism and renewed at confirmation gave me the fortitude to pull my hand away, stand up, and say, "I've had enough; I don't believe this stuff."

The witch began cursing me to my face in Spanish for disrespecting her authority. I walked out, and my lady friend that brought me followed me to my car as well. She kept trying to convince me that if I allowed the curandera to perform her rituals over me, we would both fall in love with each other and be with each other forever. Even though I was young, I knew that this lady was dangerous to my soul. She was unhinged spiritually; she was involved in the occult; she was an alcoholic, promiscuous, and deeply wounded from her past sins. That was the last time I saw her, and I have never seen her since. I hope and pray that she has found the love of Jesus Christ in the Catholic Church by now because that's what she has been looking for all her life through men that have betrayed and wounded her.

Second Encounter With a Witch

I was sixteen years old, had just bought my first car (a 1975 Chevrolet Caprice Classic), and my hormones were starting to rage because I just started noticing that women were beautiful. This is a good thing because this is the way God intended for the human race to continue to multiply itself, through the union of a man and a woman. Through man and woman's complementarity, God built that desire to unite and bond with the opposite sex, and he calls us to do so in a lifelong exclusive, faithful union called marriage.

However, at that age, I was young and immature, and I had no business dating girls. My moral conscience was not properly formed, and my faith life was shallow. I grew up in the 1970s, part of the "I'm ok, you're ok, we're all ok" generation that subscribed to the idea that if it *feels good, do it.* There was a girl in high school who was head over heels infatuated with me. She would drive by my house at all hours of the day, leave loves notes on my mail box, and call my house and leave messages (thankfully, this was way before the cellphone was invented). I was not at all interested in this young lady because she was very aggressive and pushy, and I knew about her past. She had a reputation for being promiscuous, and I knew that she had a couple of abortions by the age of fifteen, and frankly, I was turned off. She was deeply wounded from a prior unchaste relationship, and I knew that she was trying to get together with me because of her emotional woundedness. I was the guy she wanted to catch on the rebound after a bad unchaste relationship. She probably saw me as a virtuous knight in shining armor. However, I was not attracted to her; I just considered her a friend, but she wanted to be more than friends. Mutual friends of ours would tell me that she really liked me and that I should start dating her and give it a try. She was a lukewarm Catholic, just like I was. I started dating her more out of peer pressure because guys in my rough barrio neighborhood were starting to call me a *fag* (a slang offensive term which means homosexual). I succumbed to the peer pressure and started dating her so that I could demonstrate that I was not homosexual. Honestly, I was intimidated by her because I knew she was sexually active and I was not. In fact, I was a virgin; I was sixteen years old, and I was not even entirely sure what a woman had below her pelvis (seriously). It was obvious that they had breasts, but the rest of the female body was a mystery to me. One Friday night, we went out on a date and we came home at about midnight; we parked in front of her house. It was pretty obvious that she wanted this relationship to move towards being sexually intimate. I felt an eerie presence in the car as we both sat there and she started unbuckling her pants. She wasn't going to take no for an answer. Suddenly, I heard somebody yelling loudly behind us (it was about 12 midnight). Talk about a horror movie. I looked behind me and there was a lady dressed in a long lacy light dress that opened like an umbrella as she ran towards us, fast. I turned on my car and before I was able to accelerate, this ugly lady with silver hair jumped on the trunk of my car and plastered her ugly face on my back window. My girlfriend yelled, "It's the witch. It's the witch." This woman hung on to my car by extending her arms in a cruciform position and was speaking and yelling gibberish; I couldn't understand what she was saying. I pressed the accelerator and drove off fast, burning rubber. She was still hanging onto my car with her hands extended and her stomach flat on my trunk with her face on my rear window. I stopped suddenly and skidded to a halt, then I pressed the accelerator all the way down and took a right turn at about thirty-five to forty miles an hour. This launched her off my car. I looked back, and she got up and started flying towards my car again; she was not running, because her feet were not touching the ground. I quickly drove to a well-lit gas station. We both stared at each other, and we were both visibly shaken by this encounter with what looked like a witch. I had just experienced my own personal horror movie. I asked her, "Who was that? What was that?" My girlfriend said, "I have seen her before. The neighbors say she lives in Veterans Park and comes out at night to roam the neighborhoods." I felt a very evil presence in my car still. We went and grabbed a soda at a nearby Denny's. We waited there about an hour. I took her home at about 1 a.m. and never dated her again.

Third Encounter With a Witch

I dropped off my children at their school at 7:45 a.m. I parked my car and watched them run off to their respective classrooms. Then I went inside the church to pay Our Lord Jesus Christ a visit in the Blessed Sacrament. I knelt down on a kneeler in front of the tabernacle and started my morning and adoration prayers to my Lord. We Catholics actually believe that God is present in three places because God is omnipresent. We believe he is present:

- everywhere (Ps 139),
- in our hearts (Col 1:27),
- and in the Holy Eucharist (Mt 26:26–28).

When I walked into the Church, I thought I was all alone. I didn't see anybody, just me and Jesus, my Lord. As I was steeped in contemplative prayer, I heard a voice behind me speaking some unknown language that I had never heard before. It wasn't Spanish; I knew because I am perfectly fluent in Spanish. I turned around and saw a middle-aged Hispanic lady in the right back quadrant of the Church hidden in an alcove. She had several black candles on the floor in a circle. She started burning incense; she had a doll in her hand, and she was dancing around the candles. She sang in this awful dialect that sent chills down my spine; her sounds were guttural and raspy. She was dressed very shoddy, like she was homeless. We made eye contact. I said to myself, "This is a witch inside the House of God." "Zeal for my Father's house consumed me" (cf. Jn 2:17), and I walked over to her quickly and said, "Get out of her you witch. Get out right now!" She looked at me and hissed like a cat, and her eyes looked very angry and evil—they were dark—I was staring at pure evil in her eyes. I felt a surge of the Holy Spirit, courage overcame me, and I grabbed all her paraphernalia and put it in a plastic bag and threw it out the Church door.

I looked at her and said, "Repent or get out of here in the name of Jesus. Repent right now, lady, or get out." She let out an evil shriek and grabbed her bag with all her occult articles and ran out. She stopped at the door and stared at me with an evil glare and spoke in an unknown language while pointing her finger at me. I think she tried to put a curse on me. I went back in and knelt before the Blessed Sacrament and asked Our Lord and Our Lady to protect me from any evil curses she may have invoked against me. The parish priest walked in, and I told him what happened. He thanked me profusely, and then prayed a prayer of protection over me and had me recite the St. Patrick's Breastplate prayer, which is an exorcism prayer of protection against curses from witches, wizards, sorceresses, and sorcerers written in the fourth century by St. Patrick. Witches and wizards are part of the kingdom of darkness, and whatever power they draw comes from Satan, whether they know it or not.

Without a doubt, this witch had some level of demonic influence.

Fourth Encounter With a Witch

I was giving an evening conference in Spanish at Holy Family Catholic Church in Glendale, California, on a weeknight. I was invited by the Spanish prayer group. There were probably 150 people there inside the Church attending my lecture on defending the Catholic faith. It was an apologetics presentation I was asked to give. The Spanish prayer group opened up with a few praise and worship songs (called Alabanzas). I did the opening prayer and began the lecture, which was scheduled for sixty minutes, followed by a thirty-minute question and answer session.

When I was almost finished with my hour-long apologetics lecture, a lady walked into the church from the back door. She looked homeless, like she lived on the street. Her clothes were disheveled; she looked at me angrily, waved her right index finger, and yelled in Spanish, "Mentiroso, mentiroso, ven aqui, ven aqui" ("Liar, liar, come over here, come over here"). She was very aggressive, baring her teeth like a dog, and she had her hands up in the air with her fingers extended like she was preparing to scratch somebody. She then began barking exactly like a dog for about ten seconds.

Apparently, many of the locals recognized her. They began yelling, "La bruja, la bruja" ("The witch, the witch"). About 90 percent of the attendees bolted for the exits and ran out of the church; even the gentleman who was recording my talk from St. Joseph's Communications ran out of the church. I said to myself, "OK, here comes the neighborhood witch walking towards me, and she just disrupted my conference." She yelled in Spanish other insults at me and blasphemies against Our Lord inside the church. She also yelled, "Si soy la bruja, corranle corranle" ("Yes, I am a witch, run, run). Immediately, about ten Hispanic ladies from the prayer group surrounded me, took out their rosaries, and began praying it aloud in Spanish. I felt like a quarterback with a strong offensive line.

The witch screamed profanities as she lunged at me and tried to scratch my face with both her outstretched hands. I blocked her hands, and about ten Catholic women pounced on her (like a football team) and held her down. All the women and I knew this witch needed to be set free by the power of God. We knew she was under the influence of the diabolical; you could detect very strongly the evil presence attached to her. The tabernacle was only about thirty feet behind us, so we all went into full throttle prayer mode offering up rote prayers, memorized prayers, psalms, and spontaneous prayers of healing and deliverance.

The ladies sat her on a chair, and suddenly, her body went stiff like a board at a forty-five degree angle. Only her heels, the back of her thighs, and the middle of her back were touching the chair. Her body was petrified like a piece of wood. The Catholic women grabbed the holy water fonts and bathed her in holy water. She yelled in pain. Then they draped rosaries and brown scapulars around her neck while some prayed the Rosary, others prayed the Divine Mercy chaplet, and others prayed spontaneous vocal healing and deliverance prayers. I was fully engaged as well in high octane prayer which lasted about thirty minutes, nonstop.

There were a lot of curious observers at the exit doors, the ones that had run out of the Church when the witch made her grand entry. It wasn't until we started praying the Anima Christi (Soul of Christ) prayers over and over, nonstop, that she slumped down on the chair and her body returned to normal. This occurred after about thirty minutes of intensive prayer; the witch stopped screaming, blaspheming, and hissing like a cat. It was as if she was totally another person; she became calm and tranquil.

The ladies helped her stand up from the chair, and the prayer group leader (Ramona) told me, "Thank you, Jesse. We will take care of her from here." They walked her out to the courtyard, sat with her, and began sharing the gospel of Jesus Christ with her. She appeared very receptive. I had just witnessed a woman who was under the influence of demons and acting like a rabid dog become as docile as a lamb after she was subjected to a battering ram of prayer by pious Catholic rosary-toting women who were simple little lambs of God, but they were lambs who prayed like lions.

Fifth Encounter With a Witch

My pastor called me into his office one day. He told me that he was having problems with witches and sorcerers at the parish. He said that after all the Holy Masses were finished on Sundays and he had locked the doors to the parish in the evening, he was finding Santa Muerte candles in front of all the doors to the church. He said witches would also leave burning incense, dolls with needles, figurines, crystals, letters with curses against him, and other occult type paraphernalia. He would throw the items in the trash and sprinkle the area with holy water and recite prayers of blessing and protection. He said he installed security cameras inside and around the church to see who was the perpetrator that was doing this on church property.

He said that two blocks from the church was a botanica (an occult store run by witches, which is very popular in Hispanic neighborhoods). The witches who operate these botanicas call themselves "curanderas." This is a name used to identify a Hispanic woman who supposedly "heals," has magical powers, and tells people's futures by drawing upon occult demonic powers. The parish secretary was also in the office; she was a young adult who had recently graduated from college with a biology degree. She said that the lady who was vandalizing the church was the neighborhood curandera known as consejera Marta who operated the botanica two blocks from the church.

The secretary said she had seen this curandera Marta walk into the church on a weekday, stand in the back part of the church (called the nave), and run towards the sanctuary where the golden tabernacle containing the Holy Eucharist is reposed in the center and slightly elevated in a back altar. The secretary told me that the curandera ran towards the sanctuary and would bounce back as if she hit an invisible wall right where the sanctuary began. Some invisible wall prevented her from walking into the sanctuary. She did this several times. The secretary called the janitor and they went over to the church, and the witch ran out the side door.

As the secretary shared this story with me, she became overcome with fear as if she was reliving this episode once again; her eyes became watery, and she held back the tears. She said, "This is the scariest thing I have ever seen." She witnessed all of this through cameras inside the church that she monitored from the parish office. I assured her that she had nothing to fear because "he who lives in you [the Holy Spirit] is greater than he who lives in the world" (cf. 1 Jn 4:4). This brought her comfort and serenity.

I drove to the botanica, and I walked in and acted like a potential customer who was in need of occult help. I met curandera Marta and spoke briefly with her, all the while I was praying the Rosary and other prayers of protection in my mind. She was insisting that she would like me to step into her parlor so that she could heal me of my depression, but I refused and said I would make an appointment with her at a later date.

The following Sunday, I attended Holy Mass with my family, and we sat in the front row. Right after the Mass readings were proclaimed and our pastor began his homily, a lady walked into the church from the front right-side doors. It was the witch, curandera Marta. She walked in and sat on the front row at the very end.

She had with her two plastic bags full of occult paraphernalia. I could see black candles and incense sticking out of the bags. She appeared to be under the influence of a demon: her hair was disheveled and she was talking in some unknown language (not Spanish). She was looking up in the air and swinging her arms up in the air as if she were swatting flies. She was also rotating her head around as if she had vertigo. All eyes in the church were on her. My pastor kept preaching and doing his best to not let this witch disrupt his homily.

My protective instincts as a sheepdog came out, and I told my wife, "I'm going to escort her out. That's the witch curandera Marta, and she is here to steal the Holy Eucharist." My wife told me to remain calm and pray for discernment so that I could act appropriately and prudently. Holy Communion started. I stood up and allowed my three kids and wife to pass by me, and then I lined up behind my wife. I looked at the witch with my peripheral vision to make sure she remained sitting in the bench, but lo and behold, she stood up and lined up behind me.

I was extremely alert because I knew she was a witch who was here to steal the Holy Eucharist and take the sacrament back to her parlor and perform acts of sacrilege and profanity on our Eucharistic Lord. I said a quick prayer to the Holy Spirit for courage and then I turned around and said, "Pardon me, Ma'am. I have never seen you here before. Are you Catholic? If you're not Catholic, you're welcome to join us in prayer, but you cannot receive Holy Communion."

The witch told me, "It's none of your business if I'm Catholic." She was immediately confrontational. I said, "Then just take a seat and you're welcome to join us in prayer, but you cannot receive Holy Communion."

The witch said, "Who's going to stop me?" I will be honest, my lower fallen nature wanted to take over because I *knew* that she was a witch, and I *knew* that she was here for one thing: to steal the Holy Eucharist (which Catholics believe is the actual body, blood, soul, and divinity of Jesus Christ).

I fully disclosed my intentions; I told her, "I know who you are; you're a witch, and your name is curandera Marta. You operate that botanica down the street, and you're here to steal the Holy Eucharist. Not on my watch; sit down right now!"

She snarled, "Who's going to make me." Remember, I am in a packed church, and all eyes are on us as this was by now quite a disruption. I knew I had to act quickly, so I gently took her wrist and spun her around like a ballerina pirouette and now she was facing the back of the church. I gently escorted her outside of the church, and a fellow parishioner (Eddie Chavez – active peace officer) came and accompanied me as we escorted the witch outside the church. She screamed a litany of profane, vulgar, nasty curse words in English and Spanish at the top of her lungs as she was being escorted outside. When we were outside, I gently released her and said, "Go, and don't come back unless you repent and renounce your evil lifestyle, you witch."

She began cackling and said, "You won't be here all day. I will come back and steal the Sacred Host when you're gone, ha ha ha." We called the local police, and they showed up within five minutes. I pressed charges for a misdemeanor crime known as "disrupting religious services" under the

California penal code. They took the witch in handcuffs in the back of the police car and drove off.

Without a doubt, this witch had some level of demonic influence. Witches draws their power from Satan whether they know it or not.

3

WHAT THE BIBLE SAYS ABOUT WITCHCRAFT

What does the Bible say about witchcraft?

"Because it is like the sin of witchcraft to rebel: and like the crime of idolatry, to refuse to obey" (1 Kgs 15:23 DV, equivalent of 1 Sm 15:23 in modern bibles).

"You shall not permit a sorceress to live" (Ex 22:18).

"You shall not practice augury or witchcraft" (Lv 19:26).

What is a hallmark of witchcraft?

"They are rebels against the light: they do not recognize its ways; they do not stay in its paths" (Jb 24:13 NABRE).

"Hear, you heavens! Listen, earth! For the LORD has spoken: 'I reared children and brought them up, but *they* have *rebelled* against me'" (Is 1:2 NIV).

"Because it is like the sin of witchcraft to rebel: and like the crime of idolatry, to refuse to obey" (1 Kgs 15:23).

"For they had rebelled against the words of God, and spurned the counsel of the Most High" (Ps 107:11).

"Nevertheless they were disobedient and rebelled against thee and cast thy law behind their back and killed thy prophets, who had warned them in order to turn them back to thee, and they committed great blasphemies" (Neh 9:26).

I believe Satan has repackaged witchcraft to fit our modern Christian tastes but left the essence the same. Are we practicing witchcraft and don't even realize it? Being *rebellious* is as evil as witchcraft. Have we rebelled against God in the West?

Did sorcerers and witches practice human sacrifice?

"And they burned their sons and their daughters as offerings, and used divination and sorcery, and sold themselves to do evil in the sight of the LORD, provoking him to anger" (2 Kgs 17:17).

"And he burned his sons as an offering in the valley of the son of Hinnom, and practiced soothsaying and augury and sorcery, and dealt with mediums and with wizards. He did much evil in the sight of the LORD, provoking him to anger" (2 Chr 33:6).

Yes, they did!

What is witchcraft?

Witchcraft attracts people who *want to be spiritual, know the future, and lead others without submitting to God.* Witchcraft is spiritual prostitution. Witchcraft is rebellion against God coupled with a desire to be a spiritual leader and a spiritual warrior. Witchcraft is, at best, fake religion and, at worst, a diabolical one which draws its power from evil spirits (whether its practitioners know it or not).

"Now the Spirit expressly says that in later times some will depart from the faith by giving heed to deceitful spirits and doctrines of demons" (1 Tm 4:1).

What are the origins of witchcraft?

"You belong to your father the devil and you willingly carry out your father's desires. He was a murderer from the beginning and does not stand in truth, because there is no truth in him. When he tells a lie, he speaks in character, because he is a liar and the father of lies. But because I speak the truth, you do not believe me" (Jn 8:44–45 NABRE).

All supernatural power comes, ultimately, from God. Satan gives his followers limited evil power at the cost of their soul. God gives power to those who believe the truth because only "the truth will set you free" (Jn 8:32). God is truth (cf. Jn 14:6), and he will never lead you to superstition.

This is the exact opposite of Satan, who is a "deceiver" (cf. Rv 12:9) and a "liar" (cf. Jn 8:44).

"Wisdom of this kind does not come down from above but is earthly, unspiritual, demonic" (Jas 3:15 NABRE).

Witchcraft starts with a rebellious heart. Next, you become distracted by a lie, which is some occult technique that purports to give you power. Witchcraft has faith in the technique of *the craft* and not in God. This deception comes from Satan the father of lies who bestows on his followers evil power. Witchcraft will borrow words and phrases from Christianity (known as syncretism) to deceive the new practitioners, making them believe they are serving God while accessing power from demons.

Witchcraft appeals to a narcissist who has this inordinate desire to be a spiritual *free agent* without submitting themselves to God any without any regard for his Word.

Does witchcraft work?

Although Satan may be the furthest thing from the mind of the practitioner, witchcraft gives honor to Satan by the self-delusion inherent in witchcraft. There is an occasional preternatural power given to the witch or wizard, even imitating miracles (cf. Ex 7:8–11) for those who have rebelled against God and yet still want to be spiritually effective. Fr. Gabriel Amorth writes:

> It is amazing how often the Bible warns against witchcraft and sorcerers, both in the Old and New Testaments. Scripture warns us that witchcraft is one of the most common means used by the devil to bind men to himself and dehumanize them. Directly or indirectly, witchcraft is a cult of Satan. Those who practice any sort of magic believe that they can manipulate superior powers, but in reality it is they who are manipulated.[23]

"But the magicians of Egypt did the same by their secret arts; so Pharaoh's heart remained hardened, and he would not listen to them; as the Lord had said" (Ex 7:22).

"But the magicians did the same by their secret arts, and brought frogs upon the land of Egypt" (Ex 8:7).

---

[23] Gabrielle Amorth and Nicoletta V. MacKenzie, *An Exorcist Tells His Story* (San Francisco: Ignatius Press, 1999), p. 143.

How do you characterize witchcraft?

Witchcraft (whether they know it or not) draws its "knowledge from demons," and they reject the "knowledge from God" and his Word. As you climb and advance in witchcraft, Satan will give you some power for what you want here and *now,* at the cost of your soul. Witchcraft is the desire for preternatural power and the desire to manipulate the future. Witchcraft appeals to our fallen nature, our ego, our pride, and our self-centeredness. We sacrifice truth at the satanic altar of lies. We trade our birthright as sons and daughters of God for a bowl of lentil soup (cf. Gn 25:29–34).

"The magicians tried by their secret arts to bring forth gnats, but they could not. So there were gnats on man and beast" (Ex 8:18).

"Keep on with your spells and your many sorceries, at which you toiled from your youth. Perhaps you can prevail, perhaps you can strike terror!" (Is 47:12 NABRE).

Witchcraft and sorcery are enemies of the Church!

"But there was a man named Simon who had previously practiced magic in the city and amazed the nation of Sama'ria, saying that he himself was somebody great. They all gave heed to him, from the least to the greatest, saying, 'This man is that power of God which is called Great.' And they gave heed to him, because for a long time he had amazed them with his magic" (Acts 8:9–11).

Many people believed Simon Magus was a god. Peter had a wild west showdown with Simon Magus the sorcerer in public. Simon Magus began flying over Peter to intimidate him. He was carried by demons in the air. Peter did an exorcist prayer commanding the demons to let him go, and Simon Magus fell from the sky and was killed instantly.

After people heard Paul powerfully preach, the Scripture says, "Moreover, a large number of those who had practiced magic collected their books and burned them in public. They calculated their value and found it to be fifty thousand silver pieces" (Acts 19:19 NABRE).

When pagans heard the Gospel and converted to disciples of Christ, they immediately knew that witchcraft and magic were incompatible with Christianity.

Have you noticed how modern witchcraft (known as Wicca) tries to imitate Catholicism? These modern witches and wizards engage in blessing their clients, as well as cursing (for a fee of course). These witches and wizards use words like *bind* and *loose*; they prophesy, lay hands, anoint with oil, and pray over (with incantations). Some of these witches and wizards will even tell you that they are Christian; however, they consider themselves to have special hidden knowledge, understanding, and power regarding the spiritual realm. Some witches and wizards say they worship Jesus along with a pantheon of other gods and goddesses; in other words, to them, Jesus is just one of many gods. Some witches and wizards claim they reject Satan.

Satanists, witches, and wizards try to imitate Christianity and thus ensnare those that are weak in their faith (which is a large percentage of the population). These occultic groups appeal to those that want to know the future or those who are searching for some type of occult power. Because occultists practice spiritual evil, this should make us (Christians) make us (Christians) be thankful for the gifts of the Holy Spirit (received at baptism and strengthened in confirmation) and use them to build up the body of Christ.

People who are faithless and lukewarm are rebels against the Lord. They are easily deceived by sorcerers and witches!

"For this is a rebellious people, deceitful children, Children who refuse to listen to the instruction of the LORD" (Is 30:9 NABRE).

"But this people's heart is stubborn and rebellious; they turn and go away" (Jer 5:23 NABRE).

"For among them are those who make their way into households and capture weak women, burdened with sins and swayed by various impulses, who will *listen to anybody* and can never arrive at a knowledge of the truth. As Jannes and Jambres opposed Moses, so these men also oppose the truth, men of corrupt mind and counterfeit faith" (2 Tm 3:6–8).

"There shall not be found among you any one who burns his son or his daughter as an offering, anyone who practices divination, a soothsayer, or an augur, or a sorcerer, or a charmer, or a medium, or a wizard, or a necromancer" (Dt 18:10–11).

Are we getting away with practicing sorcery and witchcraft?

"The just have perished, but no one takes it to heart; The steadfast are swept away, while no one understands. Yet the just are taken away from the presence of evil and enter into peace; They rest upon their couches, the sincere, who walk in integrity. But you, draw near, you children of a sorcer-ess, offspring of an adulterer and a prostitute! Against whom do you make sport, against whom do you open wide your mouth, and stick out your tongue? Are you not rebellious children, deceitful offspring—You who burn with lust among the oaks, under every green tree; You who immolate children in the wadies, among the clefts of the rocks?" (Is 57:1–5 NABRE).

"And I will cut off sorceries from your hand, and you shall have no more soothsayers" (Mi 5:12).

"You, however, must not listen to your prophets, to your diviners and dreamers, to your soothsayers and sorcerers, who say to you, 'Do not serve the king of Babylon.' For they prophesy lies to you, so as to drive you far from your land, making me banish you so that you perish" (Jer 27:9–10 NABRE).

Witches and sorcerers fall into Balaam's error!

Balaam was a mercenary non-Israelite false prophet for hire; that is, he was a "prophet for profit." Wizards, witches, and sorcerers are hired by low information individuals, or those who don't know any better or claim to not know any better. They charge money to tell you your future, how much money you're going to make, put a curse on your ex-spouse, have someone fall in love, give someone bad luck with you, et cetera. This is the spirit of Balaam, which sells his spiritual wares for personal gain and for a hefty payment.

"Abandoning the straight road, they have gone astray, following the road of Balaam, the son of Bosor, who loved payment for wrongdoing" (2 Pt 2:15 NABRE).

"Woe to them! They followed the way of Cain, abandoned themselves to Balaam's error for the sake of gain, and perished in the rebellion of Korah" (Jude 1:11 NABRE).

"These prophets utter lies in my name, the LORD said to me: I did not send them; I gave them no command, nor did I speak to them. They prophesy to you lying visions, foolish divination, deceptions from their own imagination" (Jer 14:14 NABRE).

"But that prophet or that dreamer of dreams shall be put to death, because he has taught rebellion against the LORD your God, who brought you out of the land of Egypt and redeemed you out of the house of bondage, to make you leave the way in which the LORD your God commanded you to walk. So you shall purge the evil from the midst of you" (Dt 13:5).

"Balaam, son of Beor, the diviner, the Israelites killed with the sword" (Jo 13:22 NABRE).

Sorcerers, wizard, and witches practice lying divinations!

"False visions! Lying divinations! They say, 'The oracle of the LORD,' even though the LORD did not send them. Then they expect their word to be confirmed!" (Ez 13:6 NABRE).

"Was not the vision you saw false? Did you not report a lying divination when you said, 'Oracle of the LORD,' even though I never spoke?" (Ez 13:7 NABRE).

"My hand is against the prophets who see false visions and who make lying divinations. They shall not belong to the community of my people. They shall not be written in the register of the house of Israel, nor shall they enter the land of Israel. Thus you shall know that I am the LORD" (Ez 13:9 NABRE).

"Both these things shall come to you suddenly, in a single day: Complete bereavement and widowhood shall come upon you despite your many sorceries and the full power of your spells" (Is 47:9 NABRE).

"I will draw near to you for judgment, and I will be swift to bear witness against sorcerers, adulterers, and perjurers, those who deprive a laborer of wages, oppress a widow or an orphan, or turn aside a resident alien, without fearing me, says the LORD of hosts" (Mal 3:5 NABRE).

It is the witch in us that must die!

Modern witchcraft as its practiced in the West today has been carefully *repackaged* to appeal to the rebellious hearts of those who seek power and knowledge apart from God.

Jesus performs miracles; he does not appeal to some technique (like is taught in witchcraft).

In one instance, Jesus gives sight to a blind man by spitting in the dirt and rubbing it in someone's eye (Jn 9:6). In another encounter, Jesus touches a leper and heals him immediately (Lk 5:13). In another instance, Jesus speaks from a distance and ten lepers are healed (Lk 17:12–14). Sometimes Jesus speaks calmly when performing a miracle (Jn 4:50), and sometimes he yells when performing a miracle (Jn 11:43). Jesus was not relying on *some occult type* technique; he was relying on his Father and submission to his Father (Jn 8:28–29). The specifics of *how* miracles were performed by Our Lord varied. It is almost as if God was trying to make the point: trust in *me,* not in some *occult* technique.

For the Holy Spirit *never leads us* into superstition, indifference to God's will, or vainglory as we see within witchcraft.

"For thou hast rejected thy people, the house of Jacob, because they are full of diviners from the east and of soothsayers like the Philistines, and they strike hands with foreigners" (Is 2:6).

When we start relying on some *occult* technique, magic, or superstition and not God, then we are flirting with witchcraft. Preternatural power may come into play through the instrumentality of a demon. But if the person doing these occult works of darkness is not yielded to God's will, then it is an act of rebellion. The rebel in all of us wants God on a leash. God must perform a trick for us when we jerk his chain. Like Satan, we twist Scripture:

> "Then the devil took him to the holy city, and set him on the pinnacle of the temple, and said to him, 'If you are the Son of God, throw yourself down; for it is written, "He will give his angels charge of you," and "On their hands they will bear you up, lest you strike your foot against a stone"'" (Mt 4:5–6).

> "Now the serpent was more subtle than any other wild creature that the LORD God had made. He said to the

woman, 'Did God say, "You shall not eat of any tree of the garden?"'" (Gn 3:1).

The eternal destiny in hell is certain for those who continue to practice witchcraft by their own free will, even if their supposed miracles are "good works."

"A good intention (for example, that of helping one's neighbor) does not make behavior that is intrinsically disordered, such as lying and calumny, good or just. The end does not justify the means" (CCC 1753).

"Many will say to me on that day, 'Lord, Lord, did we not prophesy in your name? Did we not drive out demons in your name? Did we not do mighty deeds in your name?' Then I will declare to them solemnly, 'I never knew you. Depart from me, you evildoers'" (Mt 7:22–23 NABRE).

"You shall not invoke the name of the LORD, your God, in vain. For the LORD will not leave unpunished anyone who invokes his name in vain" (Ex 20:7 NABRE).

"But as for cowards, the unfaithful, the depraved, murderers, the unchaste, sorcerers, idol-worshipers, and deceivers of every sort, their lot is in the burning pool of fire and sulfur, which is the second death" (Rv 21:8 NABRE).

"Outside are the dogs and sorcerers and fornicators and murderers and idolaters, and everyone who loves and practices falsehood" (Rv 22:15).

4

SANTA MUERTE IS
SATAN IN DISGUISE

Santa Muerte means "Saint of Death" or "Saintly Death." This new cult, which has taken Mexico by storm since the rise of the drug cartels, includes elements of both Satanism and witchcraft. This female grim reaper is not part of the Catholic communion of saints; it is a demon which has now become a Mexican folk "saint" which is directly tied into, worshipped by, and invoked by the cartels as a protectoress. The origin of Santa Muerte can be traced to Mexico around the 1960s, although some claim it comes from the Aztec and Mayan indigenous people, while others claim other origins for this destructive cult.

Although practitioners use a form of witchcraft and esoteric practices to seek favors and rewards from Santa Muerte, it only has the trappings of authentic religion. Santa Muerte has a large footprint in Mexico; its members are usually criminals, gang members, and the dregs of society. These dregs pray to her to keep them safe and protected from law enforcement as they move, sell, and distribute their narcotics and weapons. They believe that Santa Muerte can make them invisible from law enforcement. They also pray to her to take revenge of their enemies and for sexual favors.

The Santa Muerte insignia is found all over Mexico's neighborhoods and cities; it has even spilled over into the United States Southwest and beyond. Growing up, living, and working in the barrios of Los Angeles County as I did, I have seen this insignia virtually all of my life.

Practitioners of Santa Muerte call their sacred space "botanicas," which they dress up with Catholic statues and images in order to lure ignorant Catholics inside their parlor. (As you will see below, there is often a mixing of Santa Muerte, Santeria, and other pseudo-religions in these botanicas.) The Latin American bishops over ten years ago officially condemned Santa Muerte and have clearly said it is the worship of the devil himself. For me, Santa Muerte is a mockery of the Catholic faith as it blasphemes the Blessed Virgin Mary and preys upon low-information Hispanic Catholics.

This cult has its own "priesthood" of sorts called "shamans" who hold "religious" services that seem to borrow or imitate a lot of what we see at a Catholic religious service, such as the use of incense, candles, kneeling, sermons, collection of money, adorning with flowers, et cetera. They also believe that Santa Muerte possesses charismatic gifts of healing and miracles. The claim is that when Santa Muerte materializes, she often assumes the form of a feminine skeletal figure cloaked in beautiful, expensive robes. She often holds a scythe and a globe in her hands to signify her role and power in the natural order of things.

Most important to know is this: Santa Muerte is the rebirth of paganism in Mexico, which never really went away. Too many Mexican Catholics are not properly formed in Catholic doctrine, and so are easily given over to superstitious practices like the cult of Santa Muerte.

Whatever "favors" a devotee may receive or think they receive from Santa Muerte would come from a demon. Unlike in our beloved and true Catholic faith, there is no call to holiness for practitioners of Santa Muerte. Cult members are overly fascinated with the future and try to manipulate the future by their occult practices. Santa Muerte is a fake religion that comes from Satan, and God will punish those practitioners for refusing to believe in the Gospel if they know in their hearts that what they do is wrong. And it is difficult to believe that even a low-information Catholic, malformed though they may be, does not know that they are getting into something dangerous and bad when they first start dabbling in Santa Muerte.

"The coming of the lawless one by the activity of Satan will be with all power and with pretended signs and wonders, and with all wicked deception for those who are to perish, because they refused to love the truth and so be saved. Therefore God sends upon them a strong delusion, to make them believe what is false, so that all may be condemned who did not believe the truth but had pleasure in unrighteousness" (2 Thes 2:9–12).

Why, then, do so many Catholics fall into this insidious cult? They do so because for them, prayer is magic; it's like rubbing a bottle with a genie that comes out and does your bidding. On the contrary, practicing Catholics know that prayer involves no magic or genie. Rather, it is trusting in Divine Providence; that is to say, God, in his time and on his terms. That is why we pray "thy will be done" in the Our Father.

It's no wonder that the Santa Muerte cult tries to imitate Catholic Christianity, for in this way, they can deceive those whose faith is not well formed and easily recruit them. The Catholic faith stands alone, it cannot be mixed together with any other religion, especially this pseudo and evil one. A Catholic who practices the Santa Muerte religion has committed a sin against the first commandment. Those who practice the Santa Muerte religion, will not have a "Holy Death," unless they repent, confess, and have contrition in their heart.

If you are concerned about or have lost a loved one to the Santa Muerte cult, fight back. Develop an intimate relationship with the One True God who is Father, Son, and Holy Ghost. Form yourself in your Catholic faith, and go out and evangelize those weaker brothers and sisters in the faith who are being deceived (Rv 12:9) and lied to (Jn 8:44) by the father of lies. St. Paul's warning to the Ephesians applies to Mexican Catholics who are being proselytized by the Santa Muerte cult.

Let all readers of this book unite in prayer to free Hispanic Catholics from the grip of Santa Muerte and all falsehood.

"Let no one deceive you with empty words, for it is because of these things that the wrath of God comes upon the sons of disobedience. Therefore do not associate with them, for once you were darkness, but now you are light in the Lord; walk as children of light (for the fruit of light is found in all that is good and right and true), and try to learn what is pleasing to the Lord. Take no part in the unfruitful works of darkness, but instead expose them. For it is a shame even to speak of the things that they do in secret" (Eph 5:6–12).

Don't be afraid, believers will cast out demons in Jesus name.

"These signs will accompany those who believe: in my name they will drive out demons, they will speak new languages" (Mk 16:17). *This grace, power and authority is given to all the baptized believers.*

Don't be afraid, believers have power over Satan.

"For while your obedience is known to all, so that I rejoice over you, I would have you wise as to what is good and guileless as to what is evil; then the God of peace will soon crush Satan under your feet" (Rom 16:19–20). *If you live in union with Jesus Christ; that is, if you live in a state of grace you have power over evil spirits.*

"Truly, truly, I say to you, he who believes in me will also do the works that I do; and greater works than these will he do, because I go to the Father. Whatever you ask in my name, I will do it, that the Father may be glorified in the Son; if you ask anything in my name, I will do it" (Jn 14:12–14). *Let's all pray that the Lord sets Mexico free from the lies of Santa Muerte.*

"Ask, and it will be given you; seek, and you will find; knock, and it will be opened to you. For everyone who asks receives, and he who seeks finds, and to him who knocks it will be opened" (Mt 7:7–8). *Lord God Almighty, we beg you to set Mexico free from this evil spirit and evil religion.*

"And whatever you ask in prayer, you will receive it, if you have faith" (Mt 21:22). *Lord God Almighty, we pray that you drive out the cult of Santa Muerte back to the foot of the cross so that Our Lord may sentence them as he wills.*

Mother Mary has power over the devil.

"I will put enmities [total separation] between thee [devil] and the woman [Holy Mary], and thy seed [the devil's disciples] and her seed [Jesus]: she [Holy Mary] shall crush thy head [the devil], and thou [the devil] shalt lie in wait for her heel [Holy Mary]" (Gen. 3:15 DV). *Mother Mary, you are the twelve-star general (cf. Rv 12:1–5) who has been given power and authority by God to crush the head of the devil. Please crush the head of Santa Muerte under your immaculate feet.*

St. Michael has power over the devil.

"Now war arose in heaven, Michael and his angels fighting against the dragon; and the dragon and his angels fought, but they were defeated and there was no longer any place for them in heaven. And the great dragon was thrown down, that ancient serpent, who is called the Devil and Satan, the deceiver of the whole world – he was thrown down to earth, and his angels were thrown down with him" (Rv 12:7).

St. Michael is the warrior angel assigned to protect the Catholic Church. Pope Leo XIII gave us the magnificent Prayer of St. Michael, a minor exorcism prayer that parishes all across the country have recently begun praying again in response to the priest scandal. It should be known and devoutly prayed by all Catholics daily, especially those who are at work combatting the errors and dangers of Santa Muerte in their communities.

> St. Michael the Archangel, defend us in battle, be our protection against the malice and snares of the devil. May God rebuke him we humbly pray; and do thou, O Prince of the Heavenly host, by the power of God, thrust into hell Satan and all evil spirits who wander through the world for the ruin of souls. Amen.

5

SANTERIA–IS IT CATHOLIC?

I mentioned the role of botanicas in the previous chapter on Santa Muerte. Here I will explain a bit more in the context of another threat to Hispanic Catholics: Santeria.

One of the intriguing things of growing up Mexican American was learning about my religion at the supermarket. At the local grocery store in my childhood barrio, you could find a large selection of votive candles for sale, all with prayers in Spanish and English for all occasions and afflictions. San Lazaro, San Ramon Nonato, La Virgen de San Juan de los Lagos, El Santo Niño de Atocha; the list could go on. This was a colorful way to get to know Jesus Christ, the Virgin Mary, and the saints.

Most of these candles would have faces familiar to most American Catholics, but there was one candle that was hard to identify. It was called Las Siete Potencias Africanas, or "the Seven African Powers." Over various images of Catholic saints, such as St. Barbara, St. Francis, and St. John the Baptist, there were written corresponding African names, such as Chango, Orula, and Ogum. Later I came to find out that these were the names of African deities from the Cuban religion Santeria. These candles could be found at the Mexican supermarket we shopped at, in spite of the fact that there were very few (if any) Cubans living in my neighborhood.

Along with centuries-old Catholicism, immigrants from Latin America often bring to this country a taste for the occult. This can be seen even on Spanish television, where fortune-tellers and self-proclaimed curanderos (folk healers) advertise their abilities to take "curses" off of people (for a fee, of course). The center of this underground spirituality is a phenomenon becoming more and more prevalent in Hispanic neighborhoods.

Besides the ethnic grocery stores, the restaurants, and other small businesses, there was the botanica. The term *botanica* also comes from Santeria, but it has come to serve as a catch-all name in this country for any occult shop in a Hispanic neighborhood selling orthodox and not-so-orthodox religious goods. Products related to Santeria are big sellers at botanicas. Santeria is a mixture of Catholicism and polytheistic African beliefs, but they practice stuff like magic, luck, consulting spirits, and other things that the mainstream Catholic Church does not practice. These are called sins of superstition, which are a violation of the first commandment.

These superstitious cults have always existed throughout Latin America in one form or another, either in small storefronts or by street vendors hawking holy cards on the sidewalk. Aside from traditional statuary and gifts for First Communion, they will sell special soaps, perfumes, and oils for everything from finding a job to making someone fall in love with you. The names for such products are in Spanish, but the English translation for these occult items range from the ominous to the ridiculous: "Money Come to Me Soap," "I Dominate My Man Oil," "Win the Lottery Candle." These occult articles can be found side by side with an image of the Virgin of Guadalupe or a Baroque crucifix. To call these places a parallel church for the low information Catholic would not be an exaggeration. Many, if not most, of the customers of these shops are at least nominal Catholics; some are devoted Catholics who are simply uncatechized (they don't have a firm grasp on Church doctrine). People who go to botanicas are often just as likely to be sitting in a pew at Mass on any given Sunday. These stores tend to be run by folk healers who have a clientele that they help with a number of personal and spiritual problems. Some carry prescription medicines from Mexico that allow undocumented people to self-medicate when no other medical treatment is available. And, perhaps most strikingly, they serve as the primary centers of the occult for such "folk saints" as la Santa Muerte and Maximon.

Walk through any Latino neighborhood in a large city, and these figures could be spotted everywhere. The feminized Grim Reaper peaks out at you from the window of a dollar store. You will probably catch a glimpse of a mustached man in a black suit, a bag of money on his lap, a rifle in his hand, and a cigar sticking out of his mouth: this is the Guatemalan Maximon. Enter the botanica, and you will find a good selection of other questionable spirits, such as the Lonely Soul of John the Miner, the Powerful Monicato, the Coyote, Don Diego the Goblin, the gothic list goes on and on. But everywhere, it seems, you see holy Death: la Santa Muerte. In the botanica, in the dollar store, and even on the magazine rack of the supermarket, Death sells. You could even call her the unofficial goddess of the botanica— and it seems that on both sides of our southern border, her cult is growing.

This can all seem like I'm airing out our Latino dirty laundry in public, but the Catholic Church in this country should be more aware of the existence and growth of these occult establishments. On the one hand, they represent the darkest manifestation of ancient superstition: veritable dens of iniquity for sins against the first commandment. On the other hand, we must come to terms with the very un-enchanted nature of much of American Catholicism: a reductionist view of religion, the denial of the supernatural, the denial of miracles, the demythologizing of Jesus Christ. This sends Hispanic Catholics to the occult, where they claim to perform miracles right now and claim to have supernatural powers and knowledge of the future. This is part and parcel of Catholicism's treasure, but the modernists have taken or explained all of this away and given us a purely horizontal social justice religion. When I say horizontal, I mean they reduce religion merely to how we treat one another in this material world, and they want nothing to do with the spiritual aspects of the faith; that is, God and the good angels, the devil and the bad angels, spiritual warfare, et cetera. And it is only natural that humans, who are both body and soul (that is body and spirit), if they don't find reference to the spiritual and supernatural in their own church, then they may look elsewhere. I have called them low-information Catholics, but at least they believe that there is a spiritual life and those things we cannot see. That's why these occult groups become attractive to the Hispanic Catholics.

All that said, a Catholic should *not* buy from a botanica. That would be supporting the occult. Well-intentioned folks could very well be exposed to evil by entering and buying authentic Catholic articles from these places. The items sold in the botanicas could be infested or have trace elements of evil *attached to these articles*. No doubt, evil spirits lurk inside of a botanica. If you decide to purchase these good items online, make sure you get them blessed by a Catholic priest before you use them. Christian (Catholic or Protestant) sites or stores are preferable. I know some stores will sell both Catholic and protestant Christian items. I prefer to buy Catholic articles from a bona fide Catholic shop.

The solution to the problem of botanicas lies in a stronger dose of good old-fashioned Catholicism—a remedy that would benefit the entire Church. Shout it from the rooftops: "Santeria is demonic and Catholicism is the one true religion." This hybrid is superstitious and deadly to your soul.

It all boils down to the intent of the person. For many people who live in such areas, these *botanica* stores oftentimes are the only places to buy affordable religious items. Though it is preferable to buy in a Catholic or Christian affiliated store, often it is not possible. If in doubt, *and you bought religious articles at a botanica,* simply have these Catholic objects blessed by a Catholic priest and keep in mind that if your heart is pure and your intentions were sincere, you have no need to fear.

Trust in Jesus, and remember that "the light shines in the darkness, and the darkness has not overcome it" (Jn 1:5).

Many people think you can practice Santeria and Catholicism at the same time, but you cannot. The two are incompatible—mixing the two is a heresy known as syncretism. Catholicism is the pure religion given to us by Jesus Christ, the Son of God; it cannot be mixed with any other religion. Listen to what the Holy Bible says about the admixture of good and evil.

> Do not be mismated with unbelievers. For what partnership have righteousness and iniquity? Or what fellowship has light with darkness? What accord has Christ with Be'lial? Or what has a believer in common with an unbeliever? What agreement has the temple of God with idols? For we are the temple of the living God; as God said, "I will live in them and move among them, and I will be their God, and they shall be my people. Therefore come out from them, and be separate from them, says the Lord, and touch nothing unclean; then I will welcome you, and I will be a father to you, and you shall be my sons and daughters, says the Lord Almighty." (2 Cor 6:14–18)

"Santeria borrows profusely from Catholicism, and many of its practitioners even consider themselves members of both faiths. Yet Santeria is clearly a very different religion from Catholicism. Its theology is vastly different, its priesthoods are distinct from the Catholic priesthood and most of its practices directly violate Catholic teachings. The same is true for all of Santeria's 'sister religions.' Each one sports

Catholic externals but is at heart an African [pagan] religion"[24] *which is the worship of demons, whether they know this or not.*

---

[24] Gabrielle Amorth and Nicoletta V. MacKenzie, *An Exorcist Tells His Story* (San Francisco: Ignatius Press, 1999), p. 143.

6

PRACTICAL ADVICE TO STAY FAR FROM SATAN AND KEEP HIM FAR FROM YOU

But before the advice, have confidence that the battle is already won. You just have to make sure that you are on the winning team when it is "game over!"

Here is the Good News.

Problem: Satan; Solution: Jesus

Let's put things in perspective. Satan has a kingdom here on earth; it's called the culture of death, but his kingdom has an expiration date. That's good news. How do we know this? Because God tells us so!

"Rejoice then, O heaven and you that dwell therein! But woe to you, O earth and sea, for the devil has come down to you in great wrath, because he knows that his time is short!" (Rv 12:12). *That's good news; Satan knows he is a short timer here on earth. He's on his way to death row very soon.*

"The devil who had deceived them was thrown into the lake of fire and brimstone where the beast and the false prophet were, and they will be tormented day and night for ever and ever" (Rv 20:10). *His days are numbered. In the final analysis, he loses big league.*

More Good News!

Jesus has a kingdom as well; there is no expiration date. That's good news. It will last forever.

"Behold, you will conceive in your womb and bear a son, and you shall name his name Jesus.

He will be great, and will be called the Son of the Most High; and the Lord God will give to him the throne of his father David, and he will reign over the house of Jacob for ever; and of his kingdom there will be no end" (Lk 1:31–33). Those who are part of *Team Jesus, win! Big league!*

Remember Church, we have been won by One. The next time the devil reminds you of your past, remind him of his future.

How Demons Tamper With Our Thoughts

Never forget that the enemy is *angelic*. They are fallen *angels*. The angelic nature is vastly more powerful than our puny little human nature, even though Our Lord took our nature. Angels are absolute in their goals and relentless in their actions. *They can influence our memory and our appetites, though they cannot control our wills. They watch us ceaselessly and, with their superior intellects that don't need to divide and compose, they know us in many ways better than we know ourselves.* And the fallen angels, the enemy, hate us, hate us, hate us, and work constantly to help us sin and lose the life of grace in the soul.[25]

Fear comes from your thoughts. Demons operate in the area of our thoughts. It's called demonic thought tampering. That's why we must "take every thought captive to obey Christ" (2 Cor 10:5). By having "the mind of Christ" (1 Cor 2:16), we are filled with the knowledge of God's love for us. And "there is no fear in love, but perfect love casts out fear" (1 Jn 4:18).

Listen to what the Holy Bible says about the importance of guarding your thoughts and mind.

"Finally, draw your strength from the Lord and from his mighty power. Put on the armor of God so that you may be able to stand firm against the tactics of the devil. For our struggle is not with flesh and blood but with the principalities, with the powers, with the world rulers of this present darkness, with the evil spirits in the heavens. Therefore, put on the armor of God, that you may be able to resist on the evil day and, having done everything to hold your ground. So stand fast with your loins girded in truth, clothed with righteousness as a breastplate, and your feet shod in readiness for the gospel of peace. In all circumstances, hold faith as a shield, to quench all the flaming arrows of the evil one. And take the helmet of salvation and the sword of the spirit which is the word of God" (Eph 6:10–17 NABRE).

---

[25]   "REVIEW: Manual of Minor Exorcisms – For the Use of Priests (Catholic Truth Society)," *Fr Z's Blog,* wdtprs.com/blog/2012/05/ review-manual-of-minor-exorcisms-for-the-use-of-priests-catholic-truth-society/.

The helmet of salvation guards the mind and thoughts. This is precisely where demons attack us.

It must be a terrible shock to a great many Catholic Christians when they realize that after receiving the sacrament of Confirmation through the laying on of hands by the bishop that nothing has changed, that their life style is still evil, that they are still committing the same old sins; in fact, they are still sinning just as much now as they were before they received the sacrament of Confirmation. They must wonder, "Why in the world did I ever spend two years of my life every week in CCD and get confirmed in the first place?"

But what many Catholics don't realize is that when you receive the sacrament of Confirmation, you are telling Almighty God that you really and truly want to change your life around and that you are going to do everything in your power to change. Being confirmed and receiving the gift of the Holy Spirit gives you the grace to be a soldier of Christ and turn your back on the corruption of this world. You must cooperate with God's grace; he gives you a new heart through sanctifying grace, but that new heart implies that you must change *the way you think* about most of the things in your life.

Romans 12:1–2 tells us what we must do after we receive the sacrament of Confirmation and become soldiers of Christ: "I appeal to you therefore, brethren, by the mercies of God, to present your bodies as a living sacrifice, holy and acceptable to God, which is your spiritual worship. Do not be conformed to this world but be transformed by the renewal of your mind, that you may prove what is the will of God, what is good and acceptable and perfect."

You were born again through baptism. God gave you a brand-new heart, as it tells us in the following verse: "I will sprinkle clean water upon you, and you shall be clean from all your uncleannesses, and from all your idols I will cleanse you. A new heart I will give you and a new spirit I will put within you; and I will take out of your flesh the heart of stone and give you a heart of flesh. And I will put my spirit within you, and cause you to walk in my statutes and be careful to observe my ordinances" (Ez 36:25–27).

However, here is the *key* to living the victorious Christian life. This happens when you combine that *new heart* God gave you in baptism with a *brand-new mind* that will come through a life of interior faith, prayer, study, confession, Confirmation, and frequent reception of Holy Communion. If you follow this roadmap, then you will see amazing and incredible Godly changes that will take place in your life. We call this interior conversion; this is the process of surrendering your entire life over to Jesus Christ every day in good times and in bad times. But *renewing your mind* involves two things that most people hate to do. *Renewing your mind* involves a great deal of *work* and *effort*. *Renewing your mind* takes a great deal of hard work on your part.

If you think about it, you cannot even start on your road to spiritual growth and spiritual maturity until you have a whole *new mindset*. You must *renew your mind*. *Remember that your mind* is the thing that has control over every single one of your actions. Your *mind* controls your *thoughts*. Your *mind* tells your body exactly what to do. It tells your mouth what words to speak. It tells your eyes what to look at. It tells your ears what things to pay attention to and what things to tune out. It tells your brain what to think about. It tells your entire being how to respond in every single situation.

So, until you renew and change your mind, the (1) secular world, (2) your flesh, and (3) the devil are still going to control you because your mind is being greatly influenced by these three forces constantly. You must be willing to follow Jesus Christ and put your Catholic faith into daily, minute-by-minute practice, and this will change the way your *mind* looks at everything. *The battle being waged by Satan against you is to take control of your mind*, because if Satan can control your *mind*, he will also control your heart. If you don't *renew your mind* through a life of prayer, virtue, and the practice of your Catholic faith, then you will not see any improvement in your spiritual life.

As baptized confirmed Catholic Christians, we must make a conscious effort to surrender our entire life over to Jesus Christ. That means giving Jesus complete control over your body, *heart, soul,* and *mind.* And in order to do that, you must stay in contact with Jesus Christ twenty-four hours a day, seven days a week. Everything you do has to go through and be approved by Jesus Christ. In other words, if you have a desire to have a few drinks, then first talk to Jesus about it. If you want to watch some filthy programs on TV, first ask Jesus his opinion. If you want to hang around with some godless friends, first ask Jesus what he thinks about it. He will definitely talk to you. He will talk to your *heart* and *mind.* He will talk to your moral conscience. He will talk to that part of you that wants to lead a Godly life. He will talk very loud and very clearly to everything that goes into making you a child of God.

And you have to keep on doing this until your *mind* has mastery over your body so that you overcome that sin. Take every thought to Jesus. Do the same thing with each sin—take it to Jesus. Do it with each bad memory—ask Jesus to heal it—each depressing feeling—ask Jesus to heal it. The devil wants you to take your *mind* off of God. He wants you to struggle with your problems apart from Jesus because Jesus is our strength. See what I mean about the hard work and all the effort that it takes to *renew your mind*? It is certainly not easy to *renew one's mind*.

Really, it is renewing your soul, as the three faculties of the soul are the memory, intellect, and will.

However, when you were born again through baptism and surrendered your life to Jesus Christ in Confirmation, the Holy Spirit came to live within you and strengthen you. The Holy Spirit, the Lord, the giver of life, is powerful, and his greatest desire is to help you. But you must meet God halfway; you must cooperate with his grace. He wants to see effort on your part; this effort will merit a reward (or demerit punishment). The Lord needs for you to keep the lines of communication open and to make sure that they stay open. You can do this through prayerful conversation with *him* all day long. This is called *living in the Presence of God*. Constantly listen for the Lord to speak to your heart, your *mind*, and your conscience.

Cultivate a "Conscience Void of Evil and Bad Thoughts"

"So I always take pains to have a clear conscience toward God and toward men" (Acts 24:16).

"I am speaking the truth in Christ, I am not lying; my conscience bears me witness in the Holy Spirit, that I have great sorrow and unceasing anguish in my heart" (Rom 9:1).

"For our boast is this, the testimony of our conscience that we have behaved in the world, and still more toward you, with holiness and godly sincerity, not by earthly wisdom but by the grace of God" (2 Cor 1:12).

"Whereas the aim of our charge is love that issues from a pure heart and a good conscience and sincere faith . . . holding faith and a good conscience. By rejecting conscience, certain persons have made shipwreck of their faith" (1 Tm 1:5, 19).

"Baptism, which corresponds to this, now saves you, not as a removal of dirt from the body but as an appeal to God for a clear conscience, through the resurrection of Jesus Christ" (1 Pt 3:21).

Of course, God speaks to your conscience because God the Holy Trinity lives in *you*!

God the Father is in you. "One God and Father of us all, who is above all and through all and in all" (Eph 4:6).

God the Son is in you. "Examine yourselves, to see whether you are holding to your faith. Test yourselves. Do you not realize that Jesus Christ is in you? -- unless indeed you fail to meet the test!" (2 Cor 13:5). "To them God chose to make known how great among the Gentiles are the riches of the glory of this mystery, which is Christ in you, the hope of glory" (Col 1:27).

God the Holy Spirit is in you. "Do you not know that your body is a temple of the Holy Spirit within you, which you have from God? You are not your own" (1 Cor 6:19).

And those times when you do sin, talk to Jesus about it immediately; say a heartfelt Act of Contrition. If it's a mortal sin, go to confession as soon as possible. Ask the Lord to help you understand why you committed that sin, the circumstances that bring that sin on, the root cause of that sin, the near occasion that brings you to that sin, the factors that allow that sin to walk through the doors of your life, and what steps can you take to prevent any future occurrence of that sin. And you have to do this each and every time you sin with each and every sin. And you have to do it over and over and over until you gain self-mastery over that sin.

If a believer does this, then soon the believer will begin to understand the meaning behind many verses in the Bible. Verses like 1 Peter 1:14: "As obedient children, do not be conformed to the passions of your former ignorance, but as he who called you is holy, be holy yourselves in all your conduct."

As you can easily see, *renewing your mind* is not a one-time event, but rather, it is a lifelong process. It's a lifestyle. That is why the *renewing of a person's mind* is only possible for a believer who sincerely wants to live a Godly life. Renewing of the mind can only happen to the believer who truly wants to surrender their life completely and fully over to Our Lord Jesus Christ and his Catholic Church. Renewing of the mind is only for the person who truly wants to change from vice to virtue, from darkness to light, and be in harmony with the Lord, Our God.

Renewing of the mind is not for the part-time Christian or for the Christian who obeys God only when it suits him. *Renewing of the mind* is a waste of time for those people because there is no hunger or thirst for Jesus Christ in their hearts. Jesus Christ is not the center of their lives.

So, the important thing when it comes to *renewing your mind* is to stay in a constant state of prayerful communication with Jesus Christ. You cannot take your eyes off of him for a second (cf. Heb 12:2). Not in this world. Not when sin is pressing in on you from every conceivable angle.

"No, in all these things we conquer overwhelmingly through him who loved us" (Rom 8:37).

God is not picking on you, he is making you holy. Sometimes struggles are exactly what we need in our lives. If God allowed us to go through our lives without any obstacles, it would cripple us. We would not be as strong as what we could have been. The Christian is no stranger to danger or suffering.

As Christians, we need to set our face like flint against the world and feel the fire in our face and be not afraid, for our God is a mighty King. Being a Christian is a choice, it's a challenge and it requires change! If you were accused and arrested for being a Christian, would there be sufficient evidence to convict you?

The three Cs of a Christian warrior are:

- conditioning (good works),
- concentration (prayer),
- and ability to be coached (obedience).

To live like a Christian, you must practice being one. No pain, no gain; no guts, no glory. Christians never take the easy way out. We pay the price. Victory belongs to the most persevering.

Your *mind*, how you think, is crucial to your faith in Jesus Christ. A good way to *renew your mind* is to meditate often on the following text of Scripture:

> Rejoice in the Lord always; again I will say, Rejoice. Let all men know your forbearance. The Lord is at hand. Have no anxiety about anything, but in everything by prayer and supplication with thanksgiving let your requests be made known to God. And the peace of God, which passes all understanding, will keep your hearts and your minds in Christ Jesus. Finally, brethren, whatever is true, whatever is honorable, whatever is just, whatever is pure, whatever is lovely, whatever is gracious, if there is any excellence, if there is anything worthy of praise, think about these things. What you have learned and received and heard and seen in me, do; and the God of peace will be with you. (Phil 4:4–9)

Guard Your Thoughts

"We destroy arguments and every proud obstacle to the knowledge of God, and take every thought captive to obey Christ" (2 Cor 10:5).

Thought is the rudder of life. As Ralph Waldo Emerson wrote, "Sow a *thought* – reap an action, Sow an action – reap a habit, Sow a habit – reap a character, Sow a character – reap a destiny."

Priests of today also have wonderful advice concerning guarding our thoughts and minds. Monsignor Charles Pope reminds us of the importance of extending mercy to others: "Mercy is a tactic of battle, Satan would 'love' nothing more than for us to hold grudges and intensify our divisions through prideful resistance. He would prefer that we despair of God's mercy or despair. . . . Thus mercy is a tool of tactical genius; it breaks the cycle of negativity and sin and robs Satan of victories and of souls, snatching them back from the downward spiral of anger and despair."[26]

Fr. Edward Broom, OMV, reminds us that frequent reception of the Eucharist can help us to keep our thoughts pure:

> Of the greatest importance in safeguarding the virtue of chastity is our relation to Jesus in the most Holy Eucharist. The Holy Eucharist is really, truly and substantially the Body, Blood, Soul and Divinity of Jesus, the Son of the living God. When we receive Jesus in Holy Communion we receive all of the following— His totality! We receive the mind of Jesus, with His memory that purifies our possibly dirty thoughts. We receive Jesus' Blood that circulates through our entire body, rushing through our veins and arteries. We receive the most Sacred Heart of Jesus with His most noble of sentiments; even more, we receive the absolute purity of the most Sacred Heart of Jesus. If you like, every Holy Communion well-received results

---

[26]   "An Early Lenten Meditation on Spiritual Warfare," *Community in Mission*, February 11, 2016, blog.adw.org/2016/02/an-early-lenten-meditation-on-spiritual-warfare/.

in receiving a spiritual Heart-transplant. As St. Paul says, "For 'who has known the mind of the Lord, so as to counsel him?' But we have the mind of Christ" (1 Cor 2:16).[27]

Our Church is chock full of wisdom which we could spend a lifetime studying and learning. For example, Saint Faustina Kowalska had an encounter with the Lord Jesus. He drew close to the saint and wrapped a golden sash around her waist. This symbolized a gift that he generously bestowed upon the saint—the gift of perfect chastity. *Her flesh would be totally submissive to her mind and spirit and no longer would she experience indecent thoughts. Jesus would be the center of her life, her all and all.* However, there is an additional very important note. Saint Faustina said that she had been begging Our Lady for this gift for a long time! Therefore, it was through the intercession of the Blessed Virgin Mary that Saint Faustina acquired this marvelous gift of perfect chastity. Let us all turn to the most pure and Immaculate Heart of Mary and beg for purity of mind, heart, body, soul, and even intention. Let us beg Mary most Holy for the grace to live out this sublime Beatitude that Jesus taught us: "Blessed are the pure of heart for they will see God" (Mt 5:8). Let us live out purity in this life so as to contemplate the beauty of the Blessed Trinity—with Our Lady, the angels, and saints—for all eternity! Amen.[28]

---

[27]   Edward Broom, ed., "Ten Ways to Win the Battle for Purity," *Catholic Exchange*, June 1, 2018, catholicexchange.com/10-ways-to-win-the-battle-for-purity.

[28]   Ibid.

St. Thomas More said, "Occupy your minds with good thoughts, or the enemy will fill them with bad ones. Unoccupied, your mind cannot be."[29]

St. Isaiah the Hermit (AD 488) sums up for us the grace of meditation:

> Meditation melts our evil thoughts and withers the passions of the soul; it enlightens our mind, makes the understanding radiant, and fills the heart with joy. Meditation wounds demons, and drives away thoughts of wickedness. Meditation is a mirror for the mind and light for the conscience; it tames lust, calms fury, dispels wrath, drives away bitterness, and puts irritability to flight. Meditation illuminates the mind and expels laziness. From it is born the tenderness that warms and melts the soul.

Saint Isaak of Syria instructs us not to try to fight the devil head-on when he tries to put bad thoughts into your mind; instead, flee to prayer! "Do not oppose head-on thoughts that the enemy sows in your mind. Instead, cut off all conversation with them by prayer to God."

Returning to a modern-day priest, let us consider what Fr. Chad Ripperger, one of the outstanding authorities on spiritual warfare, had to say in a conference dedicated to that topic: "Demons don't know the future; they don't know your mind or intellect or will. Demons can put thoughts in your mind and then they can surmise what's in your mind.

---

[29]   "Catholic Quotes on Diligence," *SPIRITUAL ELEMENT WITHIN US*, October 3, 2017, spiritualelementblog.wordpress.com/2017/10/03/catholic-quotes-on-diligence/.

They cannot make a prophetic prediction. Demons do not have access to your will, that's always under your control."[30] Elsewhere, he has written:

> In the psychological realm, the primary way the angels and demons affect man is by moving his imagination. They do so by causing a motion in the imagination which begets a phantasm (i.e. ghost, illusion, apparition) in the imagination. St. Thomas Aquinas observes that this occurs by the angels and demons forming an image in the imagination by moving the bodily organ. Yet, they can only cause a phantasm which has something prior in memory, i.e. they must use prior sense data. While they can form phantasms which we have never seen before, nevertheless, they must use the data stored in memory to create a new image. . . . Since the data must be stored somewhere, normally this is to be understood as the data stored in memory since it is the only faculty that can store sense data. This means that the angels and demons can use our past sense experience.[31]

"As for the angels, it is a way to incite us to do the right thing by moving our memory to place something in the imagination which corresponds to joy or something of this sort when we experienced doing the right thing. Moreover, they can help us to remember what we have been taught

---

30   Chad Ripperger, "Spiritual Warfare," Conference on Spiritual Warfare, February 19, 2012, Hollywood, Holy Family Theater.

31   Chad Ripperger, *Introduction to the Science of Mental Health* (Sensus Traditionis Press, 2013), pg. 534.

so that we will be moved to do the right thing. This is why devotion to the guardian angels . . . must be fostered"[32] by all the faithful.

"The angels can assist in calling to mind those things which will aid us"[33] in overcoming our bad moral habits. "With respect to the demonic, our memory is a minefield so to speak. The demons can use our past experiences against us by moving the memory (i.e. by moving the bodily organ) to recall past sins so that they can form a temptation for us. This is why experienced spiritual writers often warned against sin because the remembrance of the sin can be used against us. . . . Two things must be done to block the demonic in this respect: (1) avoid sin as much as possible so that they do not have the sense data to use against the directee (or psychologist for that matter) and (2) do those things which will merit the grace of forgetfulness. St. Thomas Aquinas is clear that the angels and demons cannot create sense data in our minds that is not there."[34]

The relationship between sin and the impact it has in our memory cannot be ignored. Everything we do in our lives will either dispose us to vice or virtue. The good or bad angels can lead us to doing good or bad. It depends on us and what we are willing to do with the free will God gave us. It is a choice that we must make every day in regard to which master we serve. Will it be God, the devil, or ourselves?

---

[32]   Ibid., 535.
[33]   Ibid.
[34]   Ibid.

Positive First Thoughts Are a Key to Grace Which Guards Us Against Satan

Michael H. Brown tells us of the importance of "first thoughts":

> It is critical in this walk called life to have good "first thoughts." You need to always start out in a positive frame of mind. If you don't, there will be trouble later, on the other side, during a review of your life (and thoughts). . . . If you want to find favor and peace, get into the habit of making your "first thoughts" positive ones—finding the good, the Godly, the worth, in everyone. Keep trained on that and you will accomplish far more than you ever thought you could. Your spirit, at peace, will know it. Your spirit will find rest. When we remove the barrier of negativity, love flows in abundance, and love guides and covers over a multitude of sins. Dislike does the opposite. Criticality reverses the blessing.[35]

To resist the temptations of ordinary demonic activity, the book *Manual for Warfare* by Dr. Paul Thigpen points out, we must guard our *thoughts* closely and reject any that lead to sin. The spiritual battle begins and ends in our *thoughts*. *The mind is the battlefield*. To examine *thoughts* all day every day is the pursuit of he who has wisdom. Always *examine the conscience*. Make sure all *thoughts* are grounded in love but

---

[35]   Michael Brown, "THE SEVEN - BY MICHAEL H. BROWN," *Spirit Daily - Daily Spiritual News from around the World*, www.spiritdaily.org/truestlove.htm.

also reality. For the devil is the opposite: the father of lies and hate. The truth sets us free. The truth also heals.[36]

---

[36] Ibid.

7

PRAYERS

Act of Abjuration (Renunciation)

In order to break evil ties whose origins are generally occult world contacts, it is recommended that you repeat several times this following act of abjuration. You may hold in your hand a crucifix and use it to make large signs of the Cross over yourself, and say at the same time:

In your Name, Jesus, and through the infinite merits of your Blood poured during the Passion, I pray you to break any hidden ties contracted between me and the evil forces. To do so, with all my strength I renounce Satan and the sin. I renounce in particular the spirit of divination, of magic, of spiritualism (enumerate the cases); I renounce sprits (say here, one after the other, the name of the occult science, the sect, the magus, or the devil to whom you have addressed) and the evil spirit prowling around me.

Lord, Thy Precious Blood flow on me, free me of any ties, cleanse me from any ills and from any traces of sin. So that, at last free, I can glorify Thee now and forever and ever. So be it.

St. Patrick's Breastplate

St. Patrick of Ireland (fourth century) wrote an exorcism/deliverance prayer that protects us from the curses, incantations, and hexes from witches, sorcerers, and wizards.

I bind unto myself today
The strong Name of the Trinity,
By invocation of the same,
The Three in One and One in Three.

I bind this day to me forever.
By power of faith, Christ's incarnation;
His baptism in the Jordan River;
His death on Cross for my salvation;
His bursting from the spiced tomb;
His riding up the heavenly way;
His coming at the day of doom;
I bind unto myself today.

I bind unto myself the power
Of the great love of the Cherubim;
The sweet 'well done' in judgment hour,
The service of the Seraphim,
Confessors' faith, Apostles' word,
The Patriarchs' prayers, the Prophets' scrolls,
All good deeds done unto the Lord,
And purity of virgin souls.

I bind unto myself today
The virtues of the starlit heaven,

The glorious sun's life-giving ray,
The whiteness of the moon at even,
The flashing of the lightning free,
The whirling wind's tempestuous shocks,
The stable earth, the deep salt sea,
Around the old eternal rocks.

I bind unto myself today
The power of God to hold and lead,
His eye to watch, His might to stay,
His ear to hearken to my need.
The wisdom of my God to teach,
His hand to guide, His shield to ward,
The word of God to give me speech,
His heavenly host to be my guard.

Against the demon snares of sin
The vice that gives temptation force,
The natural lusts that war within,
The hostile men that mark my course;
Or few or many, far or nigh,
In every place and in all hours,
Against their fierce hostility,
I bind to me these holy powers.

Against all Satan's spells and wiles,
Against false words of heresy,
Against the knowledge that defiles,
Against the heart's idolatry,
Against the wizard's evil craft,

Against the death wound and the burning,
The choking wave and the poisoned shaft,
Protect me, Christ, till Thy returning.

Christ be with me, Christ within me,
Christ behind me, Christ before me,
Christ beside me, Christ to win me,
Christ to comfort and restore me.
Christ beneath me, Christ above me,
Christ in quiet, Christ in danger,
Christ in hearts of all that love me,
Christ in mouth of friend and stranger.

I bind unto myself the Name,
The strong Name of the Trinity;
By invocation of the same.
The Three in One, and One in Three,
Of Whom all nature hath creation,
Eternal Father, Spirit, Word:
Praise to the Lord of my salvation,
Salvation is of Christ the Lord. Amen

St. Benedict's Exorcism Prayer

Cross of our holy father Benedict
Let the Holy Cross be my light!
Let not the dragon be my guide
Begone Satan!
Never tempt me with your vanities
What you offer me is evil

You drink the poison yourself!
May we be strengthened by his presence
at the hour of our death. Glory be to the
Father and to the Son and to the Holy Spirit
Amen.

Crux Sancti Patri Benedicti.
Crux Sancta Sit Mihi Lux!
Non Draco Sit Mihi Dux.
Vade Retro, Satana!
Non Suade Mihi Vana.
Sunt Mala Qua' Libas.
Ipse Venena Bibas!
Ejus in obitu nro praesentia
muniamur. Glória Patri et Fílio
et Spirítui Sancto.
Sicut erat in princípio,
et nunc et semper
et in sæcula sæculórum. Amen.

St. Anthony of Padua Exorcism Prayer

Ecce Crucem Domini!
Fugite partes adversae!
Vicit Leo de tribu Juda,
Radix David! Alleluia!

Behold, the Cross of the Lord!
Begone, all evil powers!
The Lion of the tribe of Judah,

The Root of David, has conquered!
Alleluia, Alleluia!

Evening Prayer (1962 Roman Missal)

Visit Oh Lord this habitation and drive far from it all snares
of the enemy; Let thy holy angels dwell therein, and may thy
blessing be upon us through Christ our Lord. Amen.

Psalm 90 (DV)

Psalm 91 in modern Catholic Bibles

Qui habitat. The just is secure under the protection of God.

The praise of a canticle for David. He that dwelleth in the
aid of the most High, shall abide under the protection of the
God of Jacob. He shall say to the Lord: Thou art my pro-
tector, and my refuge: my God, in him will I trust. For he
hath delivered me from the snare of the hunters: and from
the sharp word. He will overshadow thee with his shoulders:
and under his wings thou shalt trust. His truth shall compass
thee with a shield: thou shalt not be afraid of the terror of
the night.

Of the arrow that flieth in the day, of the business that
walketh about in the dark: of invasion, or of the noonday
devil. A thousand shall fall at thy side, and ten thousand at
thy right hand: but it shall not come nigh thee. But thou
shalt consider with thy eyes: and shalt see the reward of the
wicked. Because thou, O Lord, art my hope: thou hast made
the most High thy refuge. There shall no evil come to thee:
nor shall the scourge come near thy dwelling.

For he hath given his angels charge over thee; to keep thee in all thy ways. In their hands they shall bear thee up: lest thou dash thy foot against a stone. Thou shalt walk upon the asp and the basilisk: and thou shalt trample under foot the lion and the dragon. Because he hoped in me I will deliver him: I will protect him because he hath known my name. He shall cry to me, and I will hear him: I am with him in tribulation, I will deliver him, and I will glorify him.
I will fill him with length of days; and I will shew him my salvation.